Social Literacy, Citizenship Education and the National Curriculum

The movement to raise social literacy among school pupils has become a major priority of government education and social policy. Whereas citizenship education emphasizes developing pupils with social and moral dispositions, social literacy widens the issues. This timely book looks at social literacy within the revised National Curriculum, which places an obligation on schools and teachers to promote social cohesion, community involvement and a sense of social responsibility among young people.

Social Literacy, Citizenship Education and the National Curriculum is an introduction to the social purposes and aims contained in the revised National Curriculum. It provides the theory behind the movement for social literacy as well as providing information for teachers, lecturers and policy-makers on putting the government's ideas into practice.

James Arthur is Professor of Education at Canterbury Christ Church University College and Head of the Centre for Educational Research. He is on the revision panel for NC history and is a member of the National Forum on Values in Education. His previous publications include *Schools and Community: The Communitarian Agenda in Education* co-authored with Richard Bailey, published by RoutledgeFalmer.

Jon Davison is Professor and Head of the School of Education at University College Northampton. His previous publications include *Issues in English Teaching*, published by RoutledgeFalmer. **William Stow** is a Principal Lecturer in Education at Canterbury Christ Church University College. His research interests include young children's learning in the Humanities.

Social Literacy, Citizenship Education and the National Curriculum

James Arthur, Jon Davison and William Stow

London and New York

First published 2000
by RoutledgeFalmer
11 New Fetter Lane, London EC4P 4EE

Simultaneously published in the USA and Canada
by RoutledgeFalmer
29 West 35th Street, New York, NY 10001

RoutledgeFalmer is an imprint of the Taylor & Francis Group

Typeset in Sabon by Taylor & Francis Books Ltd
Printed and bound in Great Britain by TJ International Ltd,
Padstow, Cornwall

British Library Cataloguing in Publication Data
A catalogue record for this book is available from the British Library

Library of Congress Cataloging in Publication Data
Arthur, James, 1957–
Social literacy, citizenship education, and the national curriculum /
James Arthur, Jon Davison, and William Stow.
    p. cm.
    1. Social sciences–Study and teaching (Elementary)–
    Great Britain. 2. Citizenship–Study and teaching
    (Elementary)–Great Britain. 3. Education,
    Elementary–Great Britain–Curricula.
    I. Davison, Jon., 1949– II. Stow, William, 1965– III. Title.
    LB1584.5.G7 A78 2000
    372.83'043'0941–dc21   00-055816

ISBN 0–415–22794–1 (hbk)
ISBN 0–415–22795–X (pbk)

Contents

Contributors

James Arthur is Professor of Education at Canterbury Christ Church University College and his work is located in the field of 'critical policy scholarship'. He has also developed a published record in the relationship between theory and practice in history teaching in schools. He has written widely on church education policy and has also written on links between communitarianism, social virtues, citizenship and education. He has been a member of a number of national groups including the National Forum on Education and Values in the Community, the History Task Group and the DfEE Citizenship and Teacher Training Group. His publications include: *The Communitarian Agenda in Education* (Falmer), *Teaching Citizenship Education Through History* (as editor) (Routledge), *Issues in Teaching History* (Routledge), *Teaching History in the Secondary School* (Routledge), *The Thomist Tradition in Education* (Gracewing) and *The Ebbing Tide* (Gracewing).

Jon Davison is Professor of Teacher Education and Head of the School of Education at University College Northampton. His research interests include sociolinguistics, citizenship education, and personal and social education. As well as publishing widely on the teaching and learning of English and media education, the other main area of his research and publication is teacher education. His recent publications include: *Subject Mentoring in the Secondary School* (Routledge), *Learning to Teach English in the Secondary School* (Routledge) and *Issues in Teaching English* (Routledge).

William Stow is a Principal Lecturer in Education at Canterbury Christ Church University College. His research interests include the development of children's historical understanding, and comparative study in history teaching and the development of national and cultural identity. He has published in the areas of history and chronology, and values in history, and has forthcoming publications in the area of Citizenship Education.

Preface

Social Literacy, Citizenship Education and the National Curriculum reflects our concern relating to a major priority of government education policy: the movement to raise social literacy among school pupils. The New Labour government has stamped its ethical mark on the National Curriculum for England by placing an obligation on schools and teachers to promote social cohesion, community involvement and inclusion together with a sense of social responsibility among young people. The social development of pupils is promoted by non-statutory guidelines for Personal, Social and Health Education and a new curriculum area, Citizenship. Citizenship education emphasizes a range of social skills and schools are to ensure that, through core and foundation curriculum subjects, children will learn positive social dispositions. We believe that, while developments in recent years have been positive, the proposals within National Curriculum documents are not sufficiently explored or defined beyond an evocation to 'active citizenship'. The aim of this book is to explore the meaning of social literacy for schools today and to critique the nature, purpose and role of social literacy across the school curriculum by describing not only what it is, or how it might be defined, but also by examining how it might be conducted and assessed in schools.

In Chapter 1, James Arthur introduces the concept of social literacy by tracing the history of its development and describes the context in which it might be employed within education and schooling. Dr Arthur moves to an analysis of social virtues in schools in Chapter 2 and he examines how social virtues are linked to social literacy. In Chapter 3 Jon Davison builds upon the key issues identified in the first two chapters and he extends the concept of social literacy by drawing upon the field of sociolinguistics. The chapter highlights the importance of discourse in relation to our understanding of citizenship and social literacy. Finally, the chapter includes proposals for pedagogy to develop pupils' meta-cognitive understandings that are likely to develop active and ethically empowered citizens. William Stow, in Chapter 4, looks at the curriculum context for social literacy, and argues for a stronger emphasis on social learning in the early years of education. He outlines ways in which such an emphasis can be achieved in all key stages, within, across and outside the curriculum. Service learning is the focus of Chapter 5, and in it Jon Davison examines the idea of social service and social learning in an experiential context. He proposes an approach to service learning based on a dynamic model of the school in the community that will promote learning from service and thus empower pupils and make them the committed active citizens the government envisages. Finally, in Chapter 6, the contentious area of assessing social development is explored. William Stow draws upon the discussions and recommendations of the first five chapters of our book in order to explore a new model, which provides opportunities for truly integrated assessment and learning, by having ipsative assessment at its core. He argues that normative, summative assessment of schools and children is incompatible with the stated aims of Personal, Social and Health Education.

1 Social Literacy

Towards an Understanding

Introduction

Much educational research which focuses on investigating children's roles as social actors often assumes a degree of social competence or skill and therefore concentrates on how these competencies and skills are expressed and acknowledged. The influence of parents in the socialization process is often acknowledged in the literature, but the predominant focus is on the formative role of peers and schools on social skill development. These social skills are often expressed as consisting of three inter-related components: social perception, social cognition and social performance (see Hollin and Trower 1988). Increasing emphasis has been placed on the last component, particularly in terms of outcomes. Combs and Slaby (1977: 162) define social skill as 'the ability to interact with others in a given social context in specific ways that are societally acceptable or valued and at the same time personally beneficial, mutually beneficial, or beneficial primarily to others'. Obviously, in the course of their daily lives children manifest a whole range of positive social competencies, but to reduce a study of children's social roles to the measurement of 'competencies' or behaviours which involve positive and negative consequences would be both narrow and restricting. Simply providing children with a 'social first-aid kit' runs the danger of being totally instrumental in approach: we need to recognize that there are intrinsic values within all human interaction which are difficult to ignore. Consequently, the determination of what social attributes or behaviours a child might exhibit in order to be judged socially literate is only a small part of the process and, ultimately, reductive.

Children are most certainly social beings and one of the central problems for teachers is to decide how they learn to live socially with each other and with adults. There are two distinct ways of answering this question. The first view is *normative and communal*: from their culture children learn customs that provide them with a guide to act in ways that minimize conflict. The second view is *pragmatic and individualistic*: the social order of children is created by explicit and implicit agreements entered into by self-seeking individuals to avert the worst consequences of their selfish instincts. In this last view social order is dependent on sanctions and formal agreements: rules are obeyed because they confer personal advantage on a child. In the *normative* view children are persuaded of the moral force of acting socially through their voluntary associations with others, both in their immediate circle, such as the family, and in the wider community, for example, through membership of a church or club. The child in this *normative* view will not only know the correct behaviour but will perform the role without any need for regular, conscious reference to the rules governing it. Depending on the political circumstances, in the *pragmatic* view the real possibility of coercion (physical force) could be employed by the State to ensure a degree of social order.

'Social literacy' is used in this book instead of 'social competence' as it provides a broader and more subtle approach to understanding in what ways the school curriculum plays a determining role in children's social maturation. How children develop their social literacy is intrinsically a contextual matter and is not something which can be easily traced in a linear or developmental fashion. The acquisition of social literacy is a complex process which is historically and culturally conditioned and context specific. Children learn through social practices, both explicit and implicit and become human through social interaction. Nevertheless, it is also the case that children engage in social activity before they are taught it; in other words children are disposed to be social before they learn what sociability is all about. A child may acquire some cognitive understanding of what would be desirable social behaviours in certain circumstances but be unable to translate this knowledge into behaviours or actions. The question of whether schools should be assessing knowledge and understanding of a social behaviour, or the ability to perform the behaviour, remains an area of contention. Consequently, an examination of 'social literacy' is required.

Social Education and Social Literacy

Social Education, or, more commonly, Personal and Social Education, is the traditional phrase used in schools to describe the social dimension of the school curriculum. Scrimshaw (1989: 28) defines the aims of this social education as factual knowledge combined with a commitment to desirable values and attitudes with a range of social and life skills and desirable qualities of character. In contrast, 'social literacy' has not been a phrase in general usage in British education despite the recent fashion for the proliferation of 'literacies', such as: 'political literacy'; 'emotional literacy'; 'visual literacy'; 'personal literacy'; 'media literacy'; 'computer literacy'; 'technological literacy'; and 'intellectual literacy', to name but a few of the phrases enjoying their moment in the educational literature. The new National Curriculum (1999) even refers to 'financial literacy'. In many cases such phrases are left undefined, or used in ways which display different authors' conflicting conceptions of, apparently, identical terms.

The history of social literacy can be first located in its use within the context of multicultural education in Australia in the 1980s (Kalantzis and Cope 1983). Kalantzis and Cope extended the use of the term to include knowledge about, and particularly learning from, the social sciences as taught in schools. Members of the Education Faculty in the University of Waikato, New Zealand, further extended its use to include children learning *from* the study and teaching of social studies in schools. The New Zealand national curriculum therefore speaks about children acquiring social literacy by means of a study of social studies through the social processes of enquiry, values exploration and social decision-making. The term obviously relates to the acquisition of knowledge and understanding linked to the promotion of responsible behaviour and the development of appropriate social skills. It is exactly along such lines that the Sonoma State University in the USA held a conference in 1998 entitled 'Emotional Intelligence and Social Literacy' which highlighted the behavioural aspect of social literacy. Goleman (1996) provides an account of the development of this movement in the USA.

Nearly thirty years ago in the United Kingdom the Schools Council Humanities Project and the Schools Council Social Education Project (1974) were largely underpinned by a belief that there should be a clear connection between learning *from* the social sciences in the school curriculum and acquiring social skills to function effectively within a community or society. The Social Education Project report (see Rennie *et al.* 1974: 119) declared that a fundamental principle of social education was 'that everyone needs to develop the skills to examine, challenge and control his immediate situation in school and community'. The Projects linked the teaching of the humanities and social education explicitly with the social development of children. However, the term 'social literacy' was not used by the members of these Projects. A year after the Project report Richard Pring (Elliot and Pring 1975: 8) described four aims for social education: to learn about the local society; to understand how society works; to learn to be responsible; and to have the right social attitudes. These social aims anticipated much of the current debate about 'communitarian education' (Arthur 1998, 2000 and Haste 1996). Many communitarian theorists believe that the social order rests on people's interdependence and induction into social practices through which they develop their social identity. However, these social practices, within institutions like schools, can be oppressive and lead to conformity and passivity.

The 1988 Education Reform Act effectively ended the development of social studies in schools through prescribing a range of traditional subjects and defining them in abstract academic terms. The social aspects of the curriculum were thus marginalized as academic subjects sought status and respectability in the hierarchy of academic credibility which underpinned the structure of the new National Curriculum. These core and foundation subjects were not concerned overtly with the social and practical aspects of daily life. There was a realization by many, however, that if the National Curriculum was to reflect the full breadth of the aims of the 1988 Act, which included a curricular aim to fit pupils for life and the world of work, the teaching of the social component of the school curriculum would need to be integrated in a cross-curricular fashion. Subsequently, a range of cross-curricular documentation including *Citizenship*, *Health Education*, *Economic and Industrial Understanding* was produced. Social education was therefore not completely removed from the school curriculum and the National Curriculum Council *Curriculum Guidance 3* (NCC 1990a) stated that: 'the education system is charged with preparing young people to take their place in a wide range of roles in adult life. It also has a duty to educate the individual to be able to think and act for themselves with an acceptable set of personal qualities which also meet the wider social demands of adult life.'

In the tradition that the curriculum reflects the political and social context within which it is constructed, the New Labour government has given a renewed emphasis to the social dimension of the school curriculum in its *Statement of Values, Aims and Purposes* which accompanies the 1999 revised National Curriculum. This statement includes the development of children's social responsibility, their community involvement, the development of effective relationships, their knowledge and understanding of society, their participation in the affairs of society, their respect for others and their contribution to the building up of the common good, including their development of independence and self-esteem. In addition, citizenship education is now a statutory part of the school curriculum to be introduced in 2002 in all secondary schools and primary schools who will be expected to deliver citizenship education through personal and social education. Personal, Social and Health Education (PSHE) has been made more coherent within a new, non-statutory, framework. The government seeks to promote social cohesion and inclusion within society and requires schools to provide a curriculum that will contribute to meeting specific learning outcomes which involve inculcating pupils with social and moral dispositions as an essential precondition to civic and political education. Schools will be expected to motivate pupils and encourage their participation in the political processes of democratic society. This means the development of children's self-confidence and their socially responsible behaviour, in and beyond the classroom. The framework (QCA 1999b) makes it clear that schools are expected to help 'equip them with the values and knowledge to deal with the difficult moral and social questions they face'. This stated expectation extends the idea of social literacy beyond the social sciences and beyond an enabling model of citizenship education (see p. 27). Since it embodies a vision of society, it also implies that it is as much concerned with the needs of society as it is with the needs of the individual.

The framework for Personal, Social and Health Education and Citizenship for Key Stages 1–2 and 3–4 (QCA 1999b) makes it abundantly clear that young people will be expected to learn specific social skills. At Key Stage 1, children will be expected to learn how to share, take turns, play and resolve simple arguments. At Key Stage 2, children will be expected to take increasing responsibility for their social behaviour in and out of the classroom and understand the effect of their choices on the community. At Key Stage 3, children will build on these social skills by developing higher-order skills which help them to confidently take part in aspects of the community's social life. Finally, at Key Stage 4, young people will be expected to have acquired a greater knowledge and understanding of social issues and be able to articulate and discuss these issues with each other and with other members of the wider community. It would appear that this framework proposes a linear development of social literacy without perhaps fully appreciating contextual determinants.

Nevertheless, in this framework, social literacy is perceived to be an achievement on the part of the child for it is defined as the ability to understand and operate successfully within a complex and interdependent social world. It involves the acquisition of the skills of active and confident social participation, including the skills, knowledge and attitudes necessary for making reasoned judgements in a community. Many schools already play a vital role in teaching these skills and educating children about the ability to abstract; to see the connectedness of living in community, through a socially relevant curriculum. This curriculum will necessitate children learning from the subjects being taught so that they develop social virtues and values which help them to live successfully with others, understand their rights and duties to society, and to be concerned with acting for the benefit of society. The extended curriculum of the school will also provide opportunities for children to experience how to collaborate with others and how to build communities through the contributions of the people who live in them (see Chapters 4, 5 and 6).

Social literacy is concerned with the empowerment of the social and ethical self which includes the ability to understand and explain differences within individual experiences. Robinson and Shallcross (1998: 69) have reviewed the many attempts to explain or rationalize social behaviour and have highlighted how complex the process is. They summarize their research as follows: 'Social action occurs at two levels simultaneously. It occurs at the level of large institutions which shape the nature of the social, political, economic and cultural landscapes within which individuals develop their identities and it also takes place at the grass roots level, the level of action at which we, as individuals, have the free will to make choices but largely not in circumstances of our own making.'

However, the term 'social literacy' is not unproblematic, for the means by which children acquire social literacy can privilege some over others. By using the 'right' behaviour and language in the 'right way', that is, by entering the dominant discourse, socially literate persons have avenues opened for them to the social goods and powers of society. The New Labour government seeks to use teaching and the school curriculum as a means to redress 'shortfalls' in the prior social acquisition of children so that they can be included fully within society and have access to these social goods and powers. Scrimshaw (1975: 73) described the socially empowered person as being 'characterised by the possession of a sound and detailed under-standing of himself and others, and also by his ability to behave in an intelligent way in relation to others'. It is interesting how these aims for social education are almost identical to the aims enunciated by the National Forum for Values and the Community (SCAA 1996). The Forum spoke of valuing self, families and relationships with others and these ideals are incor-porated into the new revised National Curriculum. Scrimshaw also believed that children must be able to deploy an extensive social vocabulary in a coherent and sensitive way. Chapter 3 explores the central role of language in the account of social literacy.

The School Curriculum

The school is fundamentally an agency of socialization which exerts pres-sures on those involved to accept its social values as their own. Engagement with learning will also result from an induction into 'educated discourse', success in which will determine future acquisition of social 'goods': for example, particular employment paths, higher education, power, status, wealth, and so on. David Hargreaves (1982: 34–35) in *The Challenge for the Comprehensive School* detailed how schools had lost their corporate vocabu-lary, because phrases such as 'team spirit', '*esprit de corps*' and 'loyalty to the school' had declined in favour of a culture of individualism. He berated the modern comprehensive school for not making more of a contribution to the social solidarity of society. He also believed that citizenship education must include experiential learning of the kind offered by community service. The educational goals described by Hargreaves for comprehensive schools sought to increase greater democratic participation, stimulate greater social solidarity and help resolve conflict between different communities. All three goals sit extremely well with the definition of social literacy given above. He believed that if education was to contribute to a sense of greater social soli-darity then we had to revisit the questions of what sort of society we wanted and how education could help us to realize such a society?

For Hargreaves, education had become overly concerned with the cult of the individual and the content of education had increasingly moved in a technical and depersonalized direction. Hargreaves did not think that the culture of individualism in education had been an error *in toto*, only that it had become too dominant and had ignored the social functions of educa-tion, a view he summarizes as follows: 'if an excessive and exclusive attention to social and societal needs jeopardises the education of the individual, then an excessive and exclusive attention to individual needs jeopardises those of society'. It would appear that the consequence of the modern obsession with individualism is that teachers may assume, wrongly, that the good society will be created through the education of good individuals.

One possible solution he suggested was a community-centred curriculum of which community studies, including practical community service, would be an integral part. He did not want this community-centred curriculum to become a mere appendage to the traditional curriculum, nor limited to the less able in schools. Therefore, he proposed that it should be compulsory for all and that it should consist of a core of traditional subjects organized around community studies. He argued that external examinations had far too much influence over the secondary curriculum and that this influence should be reduced in favour of increased internal assessment in schools. He believed that traditional school subjects should be more integrated with each other and that teachers should consequently develop team teaching strategies. The curriculum, in Hargreaves' model, would consist of a series of general objectives which would translate into a flexible timetable and core subjects would be reshaped into new forms and contexts.

All of this was a radical rethinking of the traditional school curriculum in an attempt to help all children, of whatever ability, to be active citizens in their communities. As Hargreaves says (1982: 144), the purpose of the school curriculum is to provide children with the knowledge and skills required for them to participate effectively in all of these different kinds of communities because 'it is when we belong to many groups and communities, and play an active role within them, that we are most likely to learn about them, and resolve, the tension between solidarity and conflict'. Schools prepare children for membership of several communities, and in anticipation of this, the school needs to offer opportunities within it for children to experience different kinds of community groupings and learn about how to resolve social conflict between them. Hargreaves admits that this is a bold vision and a daunting challenge, but believes nevertheless that schools need to increase community participation and asks: 'what other major agency apart from the school has any hope of success?'

Tom Bentley (1998), writing in a DEMOS-sponsored publication, has produced a widely publicized text on education which develops many of Hargreaves' ideas into the late 1990s. Bentley speaks of 'active, community-based learning' (1998: 30) which is aimed at developing a capacity in individuals to be responsible independent learners. He details a range of volunteering opportunities for young people, many of which are geared towards preparation for employability. He also says that young people should be given real responsibility through devolving a range of decision-making responsibilities to them so that positive learning can take place in genuine communities. Schools, he argues, should appoint 'school–community co-ordinators' (1998: 72), and should eventually evolve into 'neighbourhood learning centres' (1998: 186) which welcome every learner and 'combine the social, cultural, financial, informational and human resources of their local communities with those of a publicly funded, professionally staffed education system'. Both Hargreaves' and Bentley's proposals for the school curriculum can be firmly located within the communitarian agenda for education (Arthur 2000). Together they are really advocating that pupils should experience two types of social experience which develops pro-social behaviour – peer collaboration and adult guidance. Pupils should be involved in setting the social norms for their schools and not simply have them imposed on them. In many respects both authors' proposals are fundamentally hypothetical and even utopian. Bentley's book fails to engage with the complexities and genuine difficulties of the community projects to which he briefly refers, while Hargreaves' is an untested framework for a new curriculum. Nevertheless, both Bentley and Hargreaves were consulted by the Crick committee.

The 1990s saw a more centralized and traditional curriculum in secondary schools which was contrary to the proposals advocated by Hargreaves. Hargreaves' approach seeks to increase the solidarities in the various communities that comprise democratic society and educate them to resolve their conflicts through a school curriculum based on community-centred studies. He is critical of the progressive individualism which has led to the ethical individualism in schools and proposes that genuine individuality must be rooted in group life and result from direct experience of community life. This would entail schools being smaller in size and engaging their students with a focus on investigating their local community. The assumptions behind these recommendations by Hargreaves are that children will feel fulfilled by discussing issues in groups, that they will be more empowered, and that they will increase their self-esteem, which together will bring out their innate sociability creating a more socially inclusive society.

How then might the National Curriculum in schools advance the child's social literacy? Should all subjects on the school curriculum contribute to social literacy, and if so, how should this be specified within the subject orders? The traditional subjects of the school curriculum focus almost entirely on cognitive aspects of teaching and learning, but the knowledge and learning processes that they impart can have a value in directing activity towards desired social ends. For example, History is, above all else, about people and has an important and unique contribution to make to social education. In the primary school, History develops certain skills which can be said to be key aspects of social literacy: the ability to reflect on evidence and draw conclusions, and the ability to consider various interpretations of the same event, developing a respect for evidence. History also develops attitudes which a social being needs: tolerance of various viewpoints; critical approach to evidence; respect for the value of reasoned argument. The study of the past is increasingly set in a cultural and moral context, looking at law-making, abuse of power, introducing persecution and religious conflict, as well as ideas such as cultural interdependence, diversity of beliefs, and philanthropy. The children would increasingly be asked to consider political and social actions in a contemporary moral context. Other subjects within the National Curriculum can offer similar contributions to the development of social literacy, but there has as yet been a lack of any systematic articulation of what these contributions might be, except a brief reference in each of the curriculum subjects. Research by Holden (1999) also doubts whether teachers are prepared for these new social education demands. She found that teachers see social education as learning certain social skills and various definitions were offered. 'Something you do instinctively' was common and included everything from school playground to the school ethos.

Conclusion

Social literacy is both a prerequisite for and an essential facet of schooling. Every school will contribute to social education whether it plans for it or not. It involves learning a series of social skills and developing a social knowledge base from which to understand and interpret the range of social issues which citizens must address in their lives. It also requires a complex language usage before any political literacy can be built upon and a realization that knowledge by itself will not necessarily change human social behaviour. The National Curriculum remains dominated by cognate subject areas without any real attempt to articulate the values and beliefs which they help form in young people. Information is not enough. The values and beliefs embedded in the school need to be made visible, for the school is the social setting wherein pupils learn their social literacy. We would, in summary, agree with Piaget (1932: 134) who said, more than sixty years ago:

> Young people need to find themselves in the presence not of a system of commands requiring ritualistic and external obedience but a system of social relations such that everyone does his best to obey the same obligations, and does so out of mutual respect.

2 Social Virtues in Education and Schooling

Introduction

Social literacy, we would argue, requires a wide range of social virtues which need to be both learned and cultivated. However, there are many interpretations of what these virtues mean and some commentators would not accept this thesis. There are also tensions within contemporary educational policy that is generally committed to inclusiveness and educational opportunity for all. As a consequence the purposes of education may be limited to educational aims that all can reasonably accept. This approach to education and schooling requires to some extent a neutral stance towards competing understandings of the 'good'. In this chapter we briefly describe a broad view of the complex range of modern theories in the field of the social sciences which generally hold, in various forms of argument, that moral formation comprises the acquisition of rules and social norms of behaviour that are taken in from one's external environment. These norms and social conventions are often considered to be arbitrary and consensually determined. Social customs are seen as human inventions and in this view their general purpose is one of mutual self-interest. Utilitarian theories would advocate that we should learn social rules if they advance our interests, but not ask what constitutes our interests. Human beings, it is generally recognized, have desires which are asocial and competitive and consequently require the role of the law to restrain them. In other words, human beings need to be controlled otherwise society will be rendered chaotic. Freedom, in this view, is construed in terms of the minimum of legal constraints. This generally 'externalist' view of social rules and regulations would appear to be a feature of much liberal thinking. Carr (1991: 128) reminds us that social customs and conventions are themselves susceptible to moral evaluation 'in order to appreciate that concepts of morality and virtue are not at all reducible to or eliminable in favour of notions of social rule'. Carr suggests we adopt a more 'realistic view' (1991: 187) by recognizing that human nature exhibits 'both negative aspects which require restraint and positive aspects which deserve to be cultivated'. In Carr's view the human mind is not a *tabula rasa* and therefore human nature is not completely malleable. Newly born children provide evidence for this assertion in that they engage in social activity before they are taught it. Even infants born blind will smile though they have never seen a smile and children born both blind and deaf will laugh during play, though they have never heard laughter. Children have a natural disposition to sociability. In the end, despite many decades of effort to find a scientific grounding for human social behaviour and attitudes, we know remarkably little for certain about how and why we act as we do.

There is currently a great deal of interest in the works of Aristotle and an increasing number of educationalists are beginning to focus on the practical implications of virtue approaches to social and moral education. Indeed, the very idea of teaching the social virtues has experienced a growing revival in recent years, particularly in America (see Bennett 1993; Likona 1991; Nash 1997). In Britain, both Pring (1975) and Straughan (1988: 24) have always viewed social education as ultimately aiming at moral education, at what is 'morally desirable'. Moral goodness is the aim of social education in schools for these academics. John White (1989: 14) has gone further for he believes that children need to be taught how to regulate their appetites and be inducted into the higher-order dispositions which he calls virtues. In this he clearly follows the Aristotelian view: 'of education in the virtues, with its emphasis on acquiring judgement, on learning to respond not in ways that can easily be brought under the aegis of a set of rules, but flexibly and intelligently according to circumstances'. Carr (1991) defends virtue theory and considers that the aim of education is to acquire settled habits of feeling and choice: to educate individuals so that they have control over their feelings in life and become virtuous. Whilst he recognizes the complexity of this area, he also recognizes the importance of promoting desirable character traits in children (1991: 16). Nevertheless, the merits of an education in social virtue are not widely recognized within the teaching profession which often refuses to deal explicitly with moral and social issues because of their potentially controversial nature and a believed lack of consensus in society. This had been reflected in earlier government policy of constructing teaching as a value-free activity solely concerned with competence and standards about knowing and doing. Teachers are often suspicious of being involved in the process of moral and social education, and yet they cannot avoid involvement.

Virtues in contemporary individualistic morality, as Brian Wilcox (1997: 259) has noted, 'have been displaced from their former central position. In their stead are rules which aspire to universality. Virtues, in so far as the term is used at all, are seen simply as dispositions necessary to produce obedience to the rules.' In the last forty years virtue has certainly been displaced in the educational literature and often has been considered as an inappropriate term within education. There was a restricted interpretation of virtue and critics reduced the idea of the virtues in education to a simple 'bag of virtues' or list of virtues which were once taught, but which are no longer necessary in modern society. Critics of virtue approaches claim that previously there had been a didactic and formalistic approach to teaching the virtues which was an attempt to inculcate traditional and conventional morality in the young. Similarly there were also strong fears about indoctrination and authoritarian approaches that were believed to have the potential to create an ethos of compliance in schools, which encouraged conformity and passivity in pupils. Whilst there may have been a reaction against the strongly prescriptive vocabulary of the Judaeo-Christian moral law, overall such an understanding of the role of virtues in education is not faithful to the tradition of the theory of virtue found in Aristotle and Aquinas. Indeed, it is a distortion and gross misinterpretation of virtue itself. As Bernstein (1986: 12) reminds us:

> There is no dearth of pessimistic analyses of our contemporary social situation and totalizing critiques that end in despair. There is widespread cynicism about even the possibility of any social reform that does not have its dark side. But it is also true that there are counter tendencies, that there are deep urges and needs for solidarity, community, sharing, and reciprocal understanding. It is these fragile expressions that must be preserved and fostered if we want to keep alive the very idea of moral and social development.

Carr (1991: 252) also argues against the common view that virtues are concerned exclusively with control and discipline. Understanding what virtues are and the role they might have within education and schools is a necessary first step in unpacking the concept of social literacy further.

What is Virtue?

For a detailed understanding of virtue ethics within the British context readers might usefully consult Carr (1991) and Carr and Steutel (1999). This present chapter can do no more than summarize in general outline the meaning of virtues within the social context of education and schooling. It is generally agreed that we become human in a social context and therefore through social interaction. Consequently, each child will learn what it is to be human through engagement with social practices. In discussing the nature of virtue we need to determine how these qualities of human character we call virtues might be taught. It is also generally agreed that all children are born with potential and that these natural qualities can develop into what might be considered negative or positive traits depending on how they are socialized, especially in the early years. We could conclude then that our social order rests upon people's social interdependence. In this social context virtue is to do with certain 'excellences' in a wide range of human activity. Developing these human excellences is the Aristotelian point and direction of any individual life. Intellectual virtues are the prime concern of formal education and schooling, but social virtues are necessary as a precondition for kinds of action which are useful to society. Virtues are therefore settled dispositions or traits of character formed by and necessary to sustain a lifetime of thought and good actions (Arthur *et al.* 2000: 32ff.). Whilst these virtues are 'settled' they are not static entities and consequently need to be nurtured. Social dispositions or virtues are half-way between a capacity and an action and are positive and we need to nurture them, whilst vices are negative which need to be discouraged. We have an interest in social virtues, especially their promulgation and observance in order to maintain social order. They help people work together for common purposes and emphasize loyalty, honesty and dependability. It is why Sandin (1992: 182) argues that 'education ... has a responsibility for nurturing the virtues on which life depends. Identifying these qualities and discovering ways to teach them in a manner that is consistent with the requirement of initial reflection and academic freedom is part of the social mission of every school.' Aristotle believed that significant experience of human affairs is necessary in order to make moral evaluations or judgements and that the same virtues that promote individual flourishing also promote the community. Consequently, social virtues help adapt us to successful social relations in community. He was careful to explain that the virtues are concerned with choice and require rational deliberation and reflection.

Commenting on the implications of the work of Alasdair McIntyre for schools, Brian Wilcox (1997: 259) says: 'McIntyre seeks the restoration of an essentially Aristotelian approach in which an education in the virtues has a central place; in which my good as a person is one and the same as that of others in the human community of which I am a member. The exercise of the virtues is a necessary and central part of the good life and not simply a means to achieve such a life.' The diversified applications of the axiom 'Do not to another what you do not wish to be done to yourself', in other words, love of one's neighbour, sums up social virtue. In this sense an individual becomes happy in helping others to be happy and the good person is one who experiences pleasure in choosing to act morally. There is a right of reciprocity within this thinking which expects others who benefit from an individual's positive social practices to make a return in kind. However, there is a tension here between altruism and coercion. Society has an interest in 'enforcing' certain rules and therefore rewards and punishments become central to this scheme of things. Schools have recently attempted to ensure people observe certain rules through school–parent contracts and agreements. These contractual relations, whether formal or informal, do not depend on an entrenched moral consensus but rather on rational construction and 'negotiation'. They can encourage contractual opportunism or the search for formal flaws in the details of the contract that allows a party to secure personal advantage and to escape obligations. Such a state of affairs could lead to increased litigation exploiting 'negligence' through claims for damages and could be interpreted as a sign of increasing social distance and the weakening of internalized constraints. With pupils this 'internalization' is achieved generally through teaching and example in the hope that by a process of internalization pupils will realize that rules are 'good' and that they will accept them as their own. Children come to see the value of obser-vance of rules because they not only confer extrinsic benefits on them, but also confer intrinsic worth. Children develop a sense of self-control because they value the good opinion of others, but also because they value their own self-esteem. These rules are set by society and mediated by teachers. They are pro-social and of benefit to others. Bentley (1998: 65), another British advocate of virtue approaches in schooling, makes the obvious point that: 'Virtue, the exercise of character and the practice of ethical conduct, is built out of experience rather than intellect as a set of rules or abstract values, and, as Aristotle pointed out, such experience comes from active participa-tion in the rules and norms governing an institution or a community'. For Carr (1991: 112), 'virtues are essentially dispositions, but dispositions which are moulded by or defined in terms of certain kinds of principles, conven-tions and rules which introduce a certain sort of extra-personal discipline into the life of an individual'.

Virtuous behaviour without thinking is both a philosophical and educa-tional impossibility. It must be reflective and be exercised by individuals under prudent judgements which are essentially wise decisions made in each unique situation. Virtues require critical reflection and autonomous decision-making. Sandin (1992: 168) reminds us that the exercise of virtue 'is for Aristotle the exercise of reflective and responsible choice in the actions out of which the virtuous disposition or trait is formed'. He rejects the didactic and formalistic approaches to the teaching of virtue and empha-sizes that we should help develop practical wisdom which helps build character in pupils so that they can learn to make responsible decisions. However, the very idea of social virtues presupposes that there is a human nature and that we know what it is and that there is a human telos and that we can reach it or approximate to it. These are all assumptions which are questioned in education and Nash (1997) is a major critic of what he calls the 'Virtuecrats' or 'ministers of morality'. He summarizes their intentions as follows: you detail the desirable state of character which pupils should learn; you then help them learn through example, exhortation and training and also through the reading of certain works which specify what the virtues are and then you practise them until they become second nature. He lists some of these virtues as diligence, responsibility, civility, self-restraint, prudence, self-respect, social well-being, and the ability to collaborate with others for common purposes. Whilst he is not against the teaching of virtues, he does say that the virtues make little sense unless there is a common understanding of what human nature is and that this may ultimately be justified by a divine plan which is certain to some, but clearly debatable or false to others. Smith *et al.* (1993: 13) concluded that beyond a celebration of the virtues of tolerance and appreciation of different perspectives and hearing the minority voice it was unclear if you can teach any substantive virtues.

In contrast, according to Popenoe *et al.* (1994), social virtue is based on the following character traits: being kind and considerate, trusting and trustworthy, responsible and hardworking, honest and co-operative, and respectful of rules and authority. These virtues have a social function and are observable only via attitudes and behaviour. We are not born as reliable, trustworthy, honest, dutiful, responsible, self-reliant, considerate, decent citizens. Such qualities have to be shaped into daily habits of thought by our social experiences. Social virtue is both an individual and social achievement. The family should promote these virtues, for as Popenoe says (ibid.: 31) 'the seedbed of social virtue is childhood'. He thinks the social virtues are in decline in society as a result of family functioning and a decline in community functioning. Maley believes that 'We have to *learn* virtue and we can only learn in close and sustained association with others in social and economic activities that are important to us. Other things being equal, when social bonds between individuals and groups are strong, observance of social obligations and responsibilities is more likely' (Maley in Popenoe *et al.* 1994: 80). Voluntary organizations are important for Maley (ibid.: 106) who further states that 'the social virtues arise from, and need constantly to be nourished by, the immersion of citizens in continuing and well-ordered social institutions and organizations of a voluntary kind substantially independent of state interference or control, except as the state needs to ensure lawful relations within and between them'. The question is how can they be taught and which virtues should we teach – those that benefit the community or the individual? What are the most important virtues and who decides?

Can We Teach the Social Virtues?

How do we reach a consensus on values if one set of values is commonly believed to be as good as the next person's? 'All value systems are created equal', might appear to be the modern creed. Members of society are expected to be non-judgemental and respect other people's values, whatever they are. Values are considered to be broader than virtues and consequently the National Forum for Values in Education and the Community was mandated by the government to make recommendations on whether there was any agreement on the values, attitudes and behaviours that schools should promote on society's behalf. This consensus-seeking venture, despite the many fundamental differences within society, agreed that there were indeed some common or core social norms that society could agree on. However, there was no real discussion of the issues in society as a whole and once the task had been set that consensus was required – one was produced. The 150 members of the Forum met three times and it was divided into strictly defined groups. There was a lack of authority for the values produced other than a claimed consensus. The virtues identified are secular and it seems that moral authority is being grounded in the idea of the State. Morality is seen by the Forum as both an individual matter and as a collective concern. The list of values/virtues produced by the Forum suggests that there is a set of values or virtues by which we can judge our actions. Alasdair McIntyre (1990: 349) observes that: 'The rhetoric of shared values is of great ideological importance, but it disguises the truth about how action is guided and directed. For what we genuinely share in the way of moral maxims, precepts and principles is insufficiently determinate to guide action and what is sufficiently determinate to guide action is not shared.' Interestingly, though, the word 'virtues' made a return appearance in the Forum's deliberations and has subsequently found its way into the introduction to the rationale for the National Curriculum.

The Forum listed a number of virtues which it felt society was justified in promoting in schools. These included: to develop self-respect and self-discipline, respect for others, care for others, showing others they are valued, loyalty, trust, working co-operatively, resolving matters peacefully between each other, emphasizing justice by not harming others, promotion of honesty and goodwill in others together with integrity and truth. Both the National Curriculum and the introduction of citizenship education in schools are attempts to promote these values and virtues. Through the hidden curriculum of the school, or as part of the timetabled curriculum or as a subject in its own right, social education aims to inculcate these basic virtues. There is an element of social training involved here which promotes certain social practices as acceptable, but as long as these practices are open to modification and, above all, recognize that there is a highly complex process of interpretation and decision-making implicitly involved then it is legitimate, even necessary, to teach social virtues. These virtues will not be learned only through values clarification techniques, but by reflective and regular repetition of small actions or social practices in community. It is why increasing numbers of educationalists in America and Britain focus on virtues as the basis of teaching morality in schools.

It is argued that it is important for teachers to attend as much to the cultivation of children's natural sympathies and attachments towards others as it is for them to attend to the discipline of children's selfish instincts. Virtues should be construed as something that a child should want to attain, rather than as something they are unwillingly constrained to do. Moral thought does not operate in a vacuum and while Carr (1991: 254) reminds us that 'the modern view sometimes appears to be that no one who has already been trained in or habituated to a particular pattern of moral conduct is in a suitable position to reflect rationally on moral matters', Aristotle's view was that no one is able to deliberate about moral life *unless* they have acquired by experience and practice some clear understanding of the nature of the virtues. It is well documented that there is a correlation between academic achievement and the maintenance of a distinctive ethos and appropriate standards of behaviour and conduct. In good schools teachers explain to their pupils why virtues are important and they promote particular virtues. They create an orderly atmosphere in which pupils can grow. It is clear that a range of factors influence progress in the virtues, from the pupils' natural skills to the quality of the teaching and learning through to the climate of the school.

Education is, unavoidably, a social and moral engagement. The social and interpersonal aspects of the teaching process constitute a social and moral engagement between the teacher and the pupil. Mutual respect, obedience, co-operation and much else besides are all implicated in this teaching and learning relationship. Schools are therefore a rich source of social virtues which help transform pupils into good citizens; this socialization is especially active in the early years in the family and at school. Schools are also concerned with what kinds of persons their pupils will be and the means by which that development happens. Teachers are still a major influence on pupils and the kinds of virtues they form or develop. These social virtues are reflected in what the teacher chooses to permit or encourage, for the virtues of the teacher are clearly reflected in the life of the classroom. Teachers cannot be entirely neutral, for pupils need the example of those who are not indifferent. They need teachers who are full of enthusiasms and commitments in their teaching. Teachers are a model of what it is to be a human being for pupils. Teachers also ask pupils to change in directions selected by adults. This fact raises a number of questions: by what authority do I push for change in the lives of children and at what cost to their autonomy? Teachers need to reflect on these and other related questions, for as Kelly (1995: 136) warns, 'if teachers are not merely to be agents through whose activities the values of the dominant group in society are imposed upon a rising generation, they must learn to reflect on their practice, and to do so in the widest possible terms in order to embrace all its implications'. Whilst it can be argued that teachers need to be careful about any imposition of virtues in schools, they cannot avoid social virtues in teaching. This is why it is important that the social virtues in the act of teaching are clearly described and understood.

Assertiveness, confidence, consideration, courtesy, enthusiasm, flexibility, generosity, honesty, humility, loyalty, modesty, patience, reliability, respect and self-discipline are all among social virtues which schools are concerned with promoting. In school, pupils learn what these virtues mean and the school, building on the parental socialization, will help its pupils practise them. Schools will explain why they should be practised and how they should be practised. These social virtues are, of course, inter-related. Caring, for example, is a social virtue which comes from within the child and needs to be cultivated. It involves saying and doing things that help others, taking an interest in someone, watching over them, loving and valuing them, caring for oneself and respecting others. It is closely related to the virtue of kindness which is a concern for the welfare of others. Much of the quality of life depends on these virtues to smooth relations and develop bonds between people. Where these virtues are strong, strangers can at minimum expect not to be harmed by each other, and at best expect some assistance to be offered, if needed. Loneliness and isolation result from an absence of caring and kindness. The practice of these virtues is life-enhancing. Both in turn are related to the virtue of love which involves wanting to share with others and treating others with a special care and attention – treating others how you would like them to treat you. Schools are concerned with these values. It would be useful to examine four social virtues in more detail within the context of schooling. These are justice, responsibility, trust and service. Each of these social virtues also carries a moral message of obligation. Some would argue that they are also universal because they affirm our fundamental human worth and dignity as human beings and that it is, therefore, appropriate to insist that they are observed, taught and practised by the young in families and in schools.

Justice

Education in schools is intimately connected with justice and as a social virtue it is concerned with ensuring that people receive what they deserve and that they are treated fairly in their dealings with others. It is just for someone to receive a consequence or punishment if they do something wrong as it is just for them to receive a reward or recognition if they do something right or are making an improvement to something. Being just is also concerned with protecting the rights of others as well as personal rights. Children learn that without justice people are deliberately hurt and that some will take advantage of this and continue to hurt others. Without justice people will be treated unfairly and differently because of their sex, race or religion and innocent people will suffer. When people are just they do not separate themselves from other human beings because they look or sound different. The practice of justice is founded upon a seeking after truth rather than a simple acceptance of received opinion. Individuals think for themselves and act without prejudice by seeing each person as an individual and avoiding decisions based on whether someone is fat, thin, rich or poor. Children should be taught not to accept it when others lie, cheat or bully and should also be encouraged to avoid gossip and backbiting. An atmosphere should be developed in schools which encourages children to own up to their mistakes and accept the consequences of their actions as well as being equipped to stand up for other people's rights, including their own. What school would not see their role as being intimately bound up with promoting these virtues? Tobin (1986) found that children have a sense of fairness especially with regard to themselves and that this is not a simple cognitive matter, but involved the emotions and feelings of the child. He concluded that schools need to nourish this affective dimension of the virtues (see Chapter 6).

Responsibility

Responsibility is, in many ways, an extension of respect. In respecting someone individuals are concerned also about their welfare. Being responsible means that each can depend on another and that individuals do something well to the best of their ability – they are able to respond. Children, and adults, need to keep their agreements and ensure that things are done for others. They accept responsibility for their own actions and see this as part of growing up. When children refuse to be responsible, homework is left undone, promises are not kept, jobs are left unfinished and ultimately others become disappointed in them. When children learn to be responsible they take things seriously and carry out what they agree to do. They accept credit and correction and listen carefully to instruction on how to correct mistakes in order to be willing to accept and take on new responsibilities as they grow. In the teaching and ethos of the school, schools invariably will give great emphasis to developing a sense of responsibility in pupils.

Service

Being service-orientated means wanting to make a difference in the lives of others. It is looking for ways to help others sometimes by anticipating their needs. Children do this to be helpful, not to gain something in return. Without a sense of service people would not do anything to help others unless they were paid and for some selfish motive. Without a practical conception of service children would need to be nagged or pushed into doing things. Instead, children need to learn to look for opportunities to be of service to others – to see a chance to help and to take it and not wait until asked. Schools are often particularly good at identifying opportunities for pupils to be of service to others – through charity events and community involvement.

Trust

Trust is about relying on or believing in someone. It is having confidence in someone's ability to do the right thing. Trusting other people is believing that they will do what they agree to do or say they will do. Trusting yourself is having faith in your own capacity to learn and grow. When a child has trust in someone they know that they are never alone. Without trust a child feels that they need to control things to make them turn out right. Having trust means that children do not need to worry about the things other people do. When children trust, fear disappears and others can rely on you because you keep your word. Schools build an atmosphere in which trust is developed.

Children are evaluated against these virtues as can be seen when children return home from primary school with stars and circles of various colours and sizes on their jumpers. Schools are clearly evaluating children against the four virtues above and children are only too eager to please both teachers and parents by acquiring rewards. These rewards help reinforce the social virtues and focus the mind of the child so that they can effect both a rethinking of their behaviour and acquire the social virtues. Ideally this becomes an internal matter for each child developing ulterior motives for actions and seeing such behaviour in themselves and in others as necessary for happiness. However, the danger is that children can sometimes become anxious to compare themselves advantageously with others and, in such circumstances, if prizes are used too much then the virtues become subordinated to the desire to gain the badge. It is why Murray (1996) believes that a great deal of social education has become too instrumental in purpose and overly linked with success. Schools should have and often do have behaviour codes that emphasize these four virtues. White (1996: 60) is also concerned with these types of virtues and emphasizes that schools should create the conditions in which these social virtues can flourish and develop. For her, education in schools has explicit social aims and the virtues are part of this education.

Conclusion

If a society or community is to function effectively most of its members must be made aware of and come to observe the social virtues. The key institutions in society, such as the family and school together with voluntary associations such as unions and churches, also provide an environment in which these virtues are cultivated. Whether or not these virtues are in decline, or that we are in a 'social recession', is not entirely clear, but many point to examples of antisocial behaviour in society and lack of trust in key institutions as evidence of a decline in social obligation. Education, in this context, has provided the organized systematic initiation of the child into social codes and has been regarded as the principal route to the relative improvement of the human condition. Compulsory schooling involves a process of socialization and views the uninitiated as a threat to society. Virtues cannot be taught in the way that knowledge is taught within disciplines. If they are taught in this way then such teaching does not necessarily lead to right action. Virtues are generally formed by habit; by assisting pupils to act virtuously for the common good schools help build an individual's social identity within a particular community. Human beings are social animals who create community and the institutions of civil society such as families and voluntary associations based upon moral traditions and a social covenant. People choose freely to work together and are therefore persons known by name to each other, progressively becoming ever more interdependent with each other and developing a sense of fellowship. The teacher must decide whether he or she is to strengthen the State or the social principle. Virtues are worthwhile because they help children obtain a social literacy that is beyond mechanical response which helps them both individually and collectively. Children practise the virtues and it is through actions and reflection that they become virtuous. This is why community participation is all important.

Virtues are an integral part of teaching, reflected in what is taught and also in how teachers teach and interact with pupils. The time spent by pupils in the company of teachers is formative. Intentionally or not, teachers shape the kinds of social virtues that pupils acquire. Children do not grow up to be socially competent naturally or spontaneously; they become so only as a result of personal and community effort. Carr and Steutel (1999: 252) say: 'the insights of virtue ethics are in tune with the fairly obvious conclusions that positive moral and other human development is as much, if not more, a matter of right affective nurture and good example and support from parents and community, than of the disinterested mastery of rational principles of duty and obligation'. The promotion of the social virtues is something worth having. Social virtues are comprehensive. They are concerned with the rational and emotional development of children. The social virtues are about practices, but above all, as Carr and Steutel conclude (1999: 252), 'virtuous conduct requires the kind of sensitive independent judgement which cannot be secured by mechanical adherence to general rules or precepts'. The example of teachers is central to the development of social literacy. Schools need to regard certain virtues as not only necessary but desirable because they are the conditions that underpin the social life and build our social literacy.

3   Social Literacy and the Discourses of Citizenship

Introduction

The New Labour government's agenda for the social development of pupils is located within Personal, Social and Health Education (PSHE) and in a new curriculum area: citizenship education. In November 1997 the Advisory Group on Citizenship Education, chaired by Professor Bernard Crick, was established to provide advice on effective education for citizenship in schools. The resultant 'Crick Report' contains recommendations relating to the development of the knowledge, skills, understanding and values necessary for 'active citizenship' (QCA 1998a: 10). The Report highlights three 'mutually-dependent' aspects believed to underpin an effective education for citizenship: 'social and moral responsibility, community involvement and political literacy' (QCA 1998b: 11–13). In other words, it highlights the development of what has been described earlier as social literacy.

Thus far, we have used the term *social literacy* to describe the knowledge, skills, understandings and virtues that comprise the complex process of children's social development. While the school plays a role in this development, it can, in the words of the Crick Report, 'only do so much' (QCA 1998a: 9). Such development is also the product of the complex interactions between children and their homes, and between children and the wider community in which they grow. Drawing upon our earlier discussion of social literacy we propose a model of citizenship education that will empower future citizens as well as enabling them to participate in society, that is, the need for *critical* citizenship, not just *functional* citizenship. Further, in order fully to acknowledge the centrality of 'discourse' to 'active citizenship' (QCA 1998a: 14), this chapter extends the definition of social literacy as it has come to be described thus far by drawing upon the work of socio-linguists in relation to discourse theory. This chapter also argues that, if, as a result of the social dimension of schooling, pupils are to become truly active citizens as adults, which is the stated aim of the Crick Report, any programme of social literacy must be supported by the development of pedagogy that makes transparent the discourses which underpin: the education system; teaching and learning; National Curriculum subjects; and citizenship education. We spend some time in this chapter exploring citizenship education, not only because it has become a new National Curriculum area, but because it has been presented as unproblematic. Citizenship is presented as monolithic in the Crick Report and in the revised National Curriculum, whereas, as we show in this chapter, there are many forms of citizenship that are underpinned by diametrically opposed values. While we welcome the introduction of the subject into the National Curriculum, as presented, the model of citizenship education therein will be insufficient to develop the type of social literacy we call for in this book.

Schools and Socialization

It has long been recognized that schools help to develop in children positive social attitudes and skills, such as self-reliance, tolerance and co-operation (Mannheim 1950). A. S. Neill (1968: 224) argues that learning is 'a process of acquiring values from the environment' and while the pedagogy of Summerhill was markedly different from schools within the State education system, similar beliefs are espoused repeatedly in post-war official educational documentation. The Crowther Report (Ministry of Education 1959) makes the case that education should help young workers to gain a sense of direction in the world through focusing on questions of moral values as well as providing traditional vocational and intellectual education.

The Newsom Report (Ministry of Education 1963: 52) acknowledges that schools face 'a difficult but not an impossible task' in fostering pupils' spiritual and moral development. Therefore Chapter 7 of the Report is devoted entirely to this subject and it identifies key factors that enhance or impair moral development in school. In its chapter 'The School Community' the Report reinforces the belief that schools and parents share 'responsibility for guiding their children' (Ministry of Education 1963: 70) and proposes the strengthening of links between home and school.

Morrison and McIntyre (1971: 11) state unequivocally that home, school and community 'are the settings for social and intellectual experiences' from which pupils 'acquire and develop the skills and attitudes and attachments which characterize them as individuals and shape their choice and performance of adult roles'. The early 1970s also saw the production of two Schools Council project reports on Moral Education and Social Education aimed at further developing these facets of school life by giving pupils increased opportunity 'for more personal experimentation and greater responsibility for their own learning' (Schools Council 1971: 14).

The importance of home and school in the socialization of children is fully endorsed by Lawton (1973). In all societies, primary socialization takes place predominantly within family groupings as a 'process of inducting children into the rules, beliefs and values' (Lawton 1973: 41) which underpin an individual's primary Discourse (see p. 31, this chapter). This is a mediated world view (a version of society's beliefs and values presented by someone with whom the child identifies), but for the child this is *the* world.

Secondary socialization, on the other hand, 'deals with the internalization of *partial* realities. Knowledge is now mediated by means of an institution, or by a functionary within the institution (work or school)' (Lawton 1973: 41; emphasis in original). A difficulty for schools lies in the fact that the belief and values, which underpin secondary Discourses (see p. 31, this chapter) may be markedly different from, or in direct opposition to, a child's primary socialization. In a pluralistic society, therefore, problems of knowledge and meaning are exacerbated by a multiplicity of groups holding different perspectives of the world and of knowledge (Lawton 1973: 42). The link between academic underachievement and its relation to the difference between home and school values is well documented. (See, for example: Rosen and D'Andrade 1959; Jackson and Marsdon 1962; Klein 1965; Hargreaves 1967; Morrison and McIntyre 1971; Bourdieu 1973; Willis 1977, 1981; Ball 1981; Gaskell 1985; Abraham 1993; and Davison 2000.)

Chapter 1 showed how the inception of the National Curriculum marginalized the social aspects of the curriculum. However, towards the end of the 1980s there grew a public perception of a steady fragmentation of society, which was believed to have been caused in part by the government's libertarian economic policies. It is unsurprising, therefore, that the importance of schools in the socialization of pupils and social cohesion is reasserted in the Report of the National Commission on Education (1993), which maintains that education is the conduit through which 'society transmits its values from one generation to another' (NCE 1993: 93). The values exemplified in the Report marry well with the social virtues discussed in the previous chapter and they include 'truthfulness, respect for other people, a sense of the obligations due to the community in which we live ... and a caring attitude towards others' (NCE 1993: 93).

A renewed emphasis has been given to the social dimension of the 1999 revision of the National Curriculum for England in its *Statement of Values, Aims and Purposes* (QCA 1999b). The *Statement* includes: the development of children's social responsibility; community involvement; the development of effective relationships; knowledge and understanding of society; participation in the affairs of society; respect for others; and children's contribution to the building up of the common good, including their development of independence and self-esteem. Additionally, citizenship education will become a statutory part of the school curriculum by 2002 in secondary schools. Within Key Stages 1 and 2 citizenship education will be located in Personal, Social and Health Education, which has been made more coherent within a new, non-statutory, framework. The government requires schools to provide a curriculum that will contribute to meeting specific learning outcomes which involve inculcating pupils with social and moral dispositions that will promote social cohesion and inclusion within society. Schools are expected to motivate pupils and encourage their active participation in the local and wider communities in society. The Non-Statutory Guidelines for Personal, Social and Health Education and Citizenship at Key Stages 1–2 (QCA 1999c) make it clear that schools are expected to help equip pupils with the values and knowledge to deal with the difficult moral and social questions they face. The questions of with *which*, or *whose*, values pupils might be equipped are ignored, in favour of an assumed tacit agreement with orthodoxy. Until the latest revision of the National Curriculum, the values which underpin the National Curriculum have rarely been addressed in official documentation, beyond an evocation of 'standards'. While all 'stakeholders' in the education system might agree that 'standards' and 'values' are 'Good Things', there is still little evidence in the guidelines of rigorous engagement with the difficulties surrounding the definition of values.

Despite acknowledging that adults operate in a complex social world, the documentation ignores the complexity of the processes through which pupils' social literacy is developed. Unlike scientific or mathematical knowledge which, in the main, may be developed in the school context, children's values, beliefs and attitudes are also developed within the home and in the wider community. Indeed, some children's 'home' values may be in direct opposition to those espoused by the school, as well as being at variance with those of other children. A simplistic model of citizenship education, like the one presented in the revised National Curriculum, will be insufficient to fully develop pupils' social literacy. In order to substantiate these claims it is necessary to explore citizenship and citizenship education in some depth.

Citizenship and Citizenship Education

The social development of pupils will be supported not only by the PSHE curriculum, but also by a programme of citizenship education through Key Stages 1 to 4. In Key Stages 1 and 2 this will permeate the PSHE curriculum, while in Key Stages 3 and 4, Citizenship will be a timetabled subject from September 2002. According to Kerr (1999a), the term 'citizenship' appears to have little meaning for residents of this country. As a consequence, perhaps, there has never been very strong support for a separate subject of Citizenship to be placed upon school timetables. Nevertheless, Rowe (1997) has identified eight models of citizenship education in England that comprise, *inter alia*, aspects of the following: values development, inculcation of good habits, and knowledge and understanding of legal rights and responsibilities, and of the parliamentary system. The establishment of any curriculum subject requires curriculum planners to be clear about the concepts that underpin it. Obviously, it is for this reason that the Crick Report was produced. However, beyond an exhortation of 'active' citizenship, the Report does not explore the nature of citizenship in depth.

Therefore, we now explore the nature of citizenship in order to aid an understanding of what citizenship education might comprise.

It is possible to locate versions of citizenship on a continuum, which has the poles *passive* and *active*. *Passive*, or functional, citizenship may be the product of an education which seeks only to develop knowledge, understandings and behaviours – competence – in order to *enable* an individual to participate in society. A model of citizenship education premised upon the development of passive citizens would, in the main, comprise a content-based curriculum, aimed at developing pupils' knowledge of: legal rights and responsibilities; the electoral system; the workings of national, regional and local government; the processes of the welfare state, and so on. Its purpose would be to create citizens who could function in society by performing the roles expected of them as members of that society. Conversely, *active*, or powerful, citizenship may result from citizenship education which not only enables individuals to develop the knowledge, understandings and behaviours necessary for them to function in society as described above, but which also *empowers* individuals. Through the development of levels of *criticality*, future citizens might question, critique, and debate the workings and processes of society. Such an approach to citizenship education might produce citizens who would take a leadership role in proposing alternative models of the structures and processes of democracy.

Bentley (1998) believes that 'The practice of citizenship can best be described as a connection between the particular and the universal'. While it is possible to accept the idea that an act of citizenship is always bounded by an inter-relationship of self and other, Bentley's everyday use of the phrase 'the practice of citizenship' ignores the fact that there are many versions of citizenship. National Curriculum guidance documents for Personal, Social and Health Education (QCA 1999b), which includes Citizenship for Key Stages 1 and 2 (QCA 1999c), and Citizenship for Key Stages 3 and 4 (QCA 1999d), not only avoid the values issues highlighted earlier, but they also present citizenship as monolithic. We would argue that such a position is untenable. There are many versions of citizenship – some of which are diametrically opposed. There is a need for any model of citizenship education to be clear about the type of citizen it aims to develop.

Therefore, in order to explore the concept of citizenship, Figure 3.1, 'Versions of Citizenship' (Arthur and Davison 2000), highlights the beliefs and values that might be seen as typifying versions of citizenship. The horizontal line represents the continuum from *passive* to *active* citizenship whilst the vertical line moves up from the *individualistic* to the *normative* views of children's social development discussed in Chapter 1. The quadrants in Figure 3.1 are: palaeoconservative citizens (the upper left), communitarian citizens (the upper right), libertine citizens (the lower left) and libertarian citizens (the lower right). In a chapter of this length any characterization of beliefs and values of the various types of citizen is not exhaustive and runs the risk of appearing reductive. We acknowledge fully that there are many other values, beliefs and attitudes that might be attributed to the quadrants. Our choices have not been made with any agenda other than aiming to show that it is too simplistic to refer to citizenship as if it were not a debatable term. Similarly, the beliefs and values listed in each quadrant are not necessarily only confined to the particular quadrant in which they appear. For example, the idea of *service* would naturally exist in both upper quadrants, but the versions of service would be markedly different; that is acceptance of externally constructed and imposed rules in the upper left quadrant, opposed to collective engagement in the construction of rules in the upper right. Furthermore, we offer this figure as a means to explore the concept of citizenship and the values which underpin its varying forms, as it illustrates some of the features which might be seen as characterizing types of citizens.

Figure 3.1   Versions of Citizenship

	NORMATIVE /COMMUNAL	
Palaeoconservative		***Communitarian***
tradition		collectivism
loyalty		democracy
family		service
parochialism		collaboration
fraternity		altruism
morality		sense of community
PASSIVE		**ACTIVE**
Libertine		***Libertarian***
individualism		market forces
materialism		enterprise
permissiveness		elitism
hedonism		meritocracy
apolitical		utilitarian
	PRAGMATIC / INDIVIDUALISTIC	

Source: adapted from Arthur and Davison (2000: 15)

The following paragraphs are brief descriptions of the types of citizens that may characterize the quadrants. They are not exhaustive analyses, but illustrative thumbnail sketches.

Libertarian citizens might be seen as valuing involvement in politics, but their aim is to reduce government at every level and to increase the nature and scope of the market in the form of property rights and the sanctity of contracts. They are typically not hostile to community, but not much interested either. Libertarian citizenship education would at best be about developing the child's competence to operate successfully within the capitalist system, to understand the rules and develop the dispositions of utilitarian creativity and entrepreneurial drive. At worst, it could encourage the practice of deceit, fraud and hypocrisy that is destructive of community and lethal to democracy. The widening social and economic divisions apparent in society in the 1980s serve as an illustration of the more negative aspects of libertarian citizenship.

Libertine citizens may become marginally involved in political activities but tend to be antisocial. They are generally hostile to social institutions. Their philosophy might be described as 'Eat, drink, and copulate, for tomorrow we die'. Libertine citizenship education would be radically critical of concepts such as virtue, community, tradition, and its aim would not be to extend the common good. Instead, this type of citizenship education would engage in an on going struggle to ensure the maximum freedom for each individual with everything up for questioning and argument. At worst, this libertine approach could cause division, fragmentation and strife within community.

We have chosen the term 'palaeoconservative' for the upper left quadrant, to describe the form of conservatism which manifested itself prior to what has come to be known as 'Thatcherism': a libertarian form of conservatism. We believe this distinction is necessary in order to avoid confusion with the now more common use of the term conservatism, which tends to be used to describe post-Thatcher conservatism. It is also important to make this distinction because the oppositional location of the two quadrants clearly illustrates the debates between the Thatcherite and so-called 'Wet' versions of conservatism that clashed in the last two decades of the twentieth century. Palaeoconservative citizens are socially conservative, traditional and generally tend to be optimistic about the ability of society to manage itself free from government interference. However, they typically favour State laws to enforce traditional concepts of morality. Citizenship education for the palaeoconservative would mainly be about complying with various kinds of authority. At best this type of citizenship education would encourage dispositions like respect, responsibility and self-discipline; at worst, submission, conformity and docility.

Communitarian citizens can be progressive or conservative, for they place great emphasis on putting aside personal interests for the sake of community. They seek to balance the social good of the community against the good of the individual. Communitarian citizenship education would emphasize the role, depending on the ideological perspective, of 'mediating' social institutions in addition to schools, in the belief that Society as a whole is educative. At best, this would not restrict itself to the transmission of a set of social procedures, but aim to strengthen the democratic and participative spirit within each individual. At worst, it could become majoritarian in approach, insisting on the acceptance of the moral position of the majority in society. We would argue that it is to the best ideal of the communitarian citizen that New Labour aspires, in its revision of the National Curriculum. In this sense New Labour has an agenda which is to produce a majority of citizens who will express communitarian sentiments, in the same way that Thatcherism attempted to encourage citizens to feel at home in expressing libertarian sentiments (see Arthur 1998, 1999). That communitarianism may be progressive or conservative (or, perhaps, both) is highlighted in the debates over the New Labour government's policies on education since the General Election of 1997.

Clearly, this brief exploration illustrates that it is, perhaps, too simplistic to begin to develop citizenship education without discussing the nature of citizenship itself. Furthermore, the term 'social literacy' is not unproblematic, for the means by which children acquire social literacy can privilege some over others. By using the 'right' behaviour and language in the 'right way', that is, by entering the dominant discourse, socially literate citizens have avenues opened for them to the social goods and powers of society. The New Labour government seeks to use citizenship education in the school curriculum as a means to redress deficiencies in the prior social acquisition of children in the name of 'inclusion'. What is now more commonly referred to as the Crick Report (QCA 1998a: 14) maintains that 'discourse is obviously fundamental to active citizenship'. It is to the central role of language in the account of social literacy that we now turn.

Discourse

The work of socio-linguists James Paul Gee, Colin Lankshear and Neil Mercer enables us to develop further the concept of social literacy. Adult illiteracy is perceived to result from a lack of the skills needed by people in order to survive, or function, at a minimally determined, adequate level within society. Discussions of the level of adult illiteracy often cite causal factors related to economic or educational inequality; an individual's, or a group's, lack of social power. In reality, of course, such factors are enmeshed.

Gee (1987) proposes that individuals belong to a community and increase their social power within that community by learning and controlling discourses. Gee draws a distinction between 'discourse', which he defines as 'connected stretches of language that make sense' found within 'Discourses' (Gee 1990: 143), and Discourse, defined as: 'a socially accepted association among ways of using language, of thinking, and of acting that can be used to identify oneself as a member of a socially meaningful group or "social network"'. Gee's definition of Discourse is important in relation to our discussion of social literacy because, significantly, 'Discourse' is always greater than language ('discourse') as it encompasses beliefs, values and ways of thinking, of behaving and of using language.

Gee further proposes that an individual's *primary* Discourse is in most instances acquired through socialization into the family. The acquisition of thoughts, values, attitudes and ways of using language creates an individual's 'world view'. In terms of social development, it may be located within the *normative* view described in Chapter 1, as social engagement in this context is most likely to be one-to-one, face-to-face. Human beings develop through a process of reflection upon action: a conscious objectification of their own and others' actions through investigation, contemplation and comment (Freire 1972). Through engagement in such a process, individuals become active historical and cultural agents. Such 'becoming' is achieved through a process of 'dialogue' (Freire 1985: 49–59). One such context for 'dialogue' is in the meeting of *primary* and *secondary* Discourses.

Individuals encounter *secondary* Discourses through engagement in diverse social institutions: schools; churches; societies; clubs; through participation in aspects of popular culture, for example. Such secondary Discourses also involve uses of language and ways of thinking, of believing, valuing and behaving which may offer human beings new and different ways of seeing the world. Each quadrant identified in Figure 3.1 has its own secondary Discourse, as shown by the examples of beliefs, values and attitudes identified. Pursuing Gee's analysis, Lankshear (1997: 17) proposes that 'Education, socialisation, training, apprenticeship and enculturation are among the terms we use to refer to processes by which individuals are initiated into the Discourses of their identity formations'.

Drawing upon developmental psychology, in Figure 3.2, 'Stages of Development', Bentley (1998: 63–64) attempts to illustrate how children develop 'an emerging set of relationships' with the world beginning with 'the immediate consciousness of the self, the sensations and instincts which are felt most directly', through a 'recognition of others' which develops 'an early understanding of multiple perspectives – that other people see things differently – and the development of second order thinking, the beginnings of a capacity to generalize, to move from the concrete and immediate to the abstract and general'. He argues that citizenship development may be represented by similar stages of development which begins with the self and radiates outwards through personal relationships to communities and ultimately to society and 'the most abstract and often the most distant ring of beliefs, concepts and experiences' (Bentley 1998: 64). Mulgan (1997) views such development in terms of individuals learning the rules and principles which govern behaviour in these ever widening circles. Such knowledge and understanding may then be applied in specific instances in a range of contexts. In Figure 3.3, 'Discourses', we adapt Bentley's framework by mapping on to it

Figure 3.2   Stages of Development

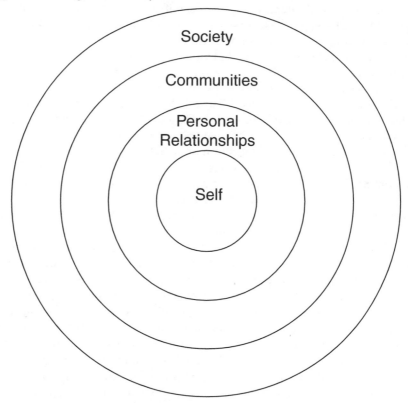

Source: Bentley (1998: 64)

an illustration of the location of primary and secondary Discourses proposed by Gee. The exploration and articulation of these Discourses would make Mulgan's 'rules and principles' visible to pupils. We would also argue that the interactions, which take place between the individual and 'the other', are at least a two-way process as indicated by the arrows in Figure 3.3. Bentley's model appears to propose that development is a one-way outward journey and as such ignores the complexities of the formation of understandings about what it means to be a citizen in society. Bentley's positioning of 'Society' at the top of the figure, instead of at the bottom, might also be read by some as an indicator of his views of the relative importance of 'Self' and 'Society'. For reasons we state later in this chapter – Bentley's close links with the Secretary of State and the Crick committee (see p. 35) – we give space to Bentley's discussion in some detail, because it would appear to provide us with detailed insight into the government's thinking in relation to citizenship education.

Schools are complex discourse communities. The language, values, ways of being and membership of various facets of the school, whether of staff

Figure 3.3   Discourses

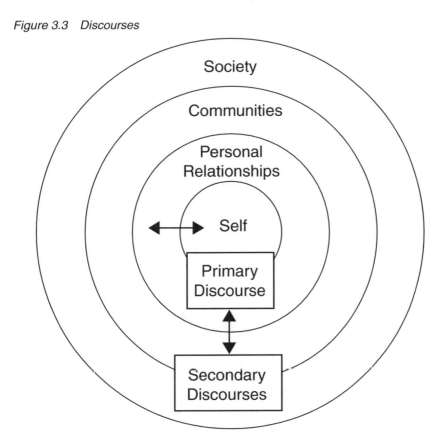

Source: Bentley (1998: 64)

or pupils, define, and are defined by, individuals' engagement with Discourses. However, although schools invariably draw up statements, or policies, concerning ethos and values in general terms, the very values, beliefs and ways of thinking which specifically underpin the Discourses of the subjects in the curriculum are rarely, if ever, made explicit. Rather, the content of subjects is 'delivered'. Similarly, the values underpinning a National Curriculum of core and foundation subjects and their relative worth are rarely examined.

Gee (1992: 25–26) defines 'powerful literacy' as 'control of a secondary use of language in a secondary Discourse'. However, powerful literacy is not a particular literacy, *per se*, but a particular *use* of literacy. Gee believes that such control over language not only enables the individual to participate in that Discourse, but that it also serves as a meta-discourse to critique an individual's primary Discourse. Furthermore, it also enables an individual to critique other secondary Discourses, as the debate in recent years between the communitarians and libertarians illustrates.

Pupils are empowered through *learning* the meta-level linguistic cognitive and linguistic skills, as opposed to *acquiring* the language of the secondary Discourse. An illustration of this distinction might be seen in the difference between slavishly following a teacher-provided, model structure to write up an experiment in a science lesson (*acquisition*), as opposed to understanding the values that underpin scientific enquiry which impose certain methodological demands upon those conducting experiments (*learning*). A pupil who has acquired the Discourse is *enabled*, while the pupil who has learned is *empowered*. Lankshear (1997: 72) sums up the importance of this meta-level knowledge as: 'knowledge about what is involved in participating in some Discourse(s). It is more than merely knowing how (that is, being able) to engage successfully in a particular discursive practice. Rather, meta-level knowledge is knowing about the nature of that practice, its constitutive values and beliefs, its meaning and significance, how it relates to other practices, what it is about successful performance that makes it successful, and so on.'

Lankshear argues that such knowledge empowers the individual in at least three ways. Firstly, the individual's level of social performance within the Discourse is enhanced, thus increasing the chances of access to social 'goods'. This mode of empowerment is easily related to success in the education system. Secondly, control over secondary language uses provides the means by which a Discourse may be analyzed to see how skills and knowledge may be used in new ways and directions *within* that Discourse. Finally, the meta-level knowledge of a number of secondary Discourses makes it possible to critique and transform a secondary Discourse. Furthermore, critical awareness of alternative Discourses allows the possibility of *choice* among them. Critical choice among Discourses, opposed to simple acquisition or rejection of Discourses without such learning and understanding, is empowerment – and it is the essence of social literacy and active citizenship. Fundamentally, the school is an agency of socialization that exerts pressures on those involved to accept its social values as their own. Successful engagement with learning through an induction into 'educated discourse' (Mercer 1995: 84) will determine pupils' future acquisition of social 'goods': for example, particular employment paths, further and higher education, and, ultimately, status and wealth. Consequently, we would argue that the development of social literacy as described here is an essential precondition for the successful preparation of children to participate fully in the life of their communities and within the wider society after they leave school.

The Challenge for the School Curriculum

Chapter 1 discussed how in *The Challenge for the Comprehensive School* (Hargreaves 1982: 34–35), the writer laments that schools lost their 'corporate vocabulary'. We would, perhaps, argue that a change in what had been the prevailing secondary Discourses of schools had resulted from a change in the dominant discourse of education. Hargreaves believed that phrases such as 'team spirit', '*esprit de corps*' and 'loyalty to the school' had declined in favour of a culture of individualism. The values underpinning the discourse of a culture of individualism might more readily be located in the libertarian quadrant, rather than the communitarian quadrant, of Figure 3.1, which would appear to be more in tune with the values that underpin Hargreaves' line of argument. Hargreaves argues in favour of schools making a contribution to the social solidarity of society, which would be promoted by citizenship education based on experiential learning through community service. Hargreaves' three educational goals for comprehensive schools can be mapped directly onto the version of communitarian citizenship education proposed by the New Labour government: to increase greater democratic participation; to stimulate greater social solidarity; and to help resolve conflict between different communities. Similarly, such an approach would have importance to the development of social literacy, as involvement in community service would give pupils the opportunity to encounter a range of secondary Discourses. It has long been recognized that community-centred schooling 'attempts to make visible connections between different homes and different cultures in a climate that respects and cherishes creative difference. It also nurtures similarities' (Wilcox 1969: 127). Integral to Hargreaves' model of a community-centred curriculum is the proposal for community studies, including practical community service. This version of a national curriculum would comprise a core of 'traditional' subjects organized around community studies, with a reduction of the influence of external examinations in favour of increased school-based teacher assessment.

Arguably, the curriculum reflects the political and social context within which it is constructed and educational legislation in the intervening two decades has constructed a curriculum that is, in many ways, the antithesis of Hargreaves' model. However, it is interesting to observe that, with the return of a New Labour government for the first time in as many years, such ideas have resurfaced and much of what Hargreaves proposes can be found in the Crick Report. This fact is, perhaps, unsurprising when we note that Professor Hargreaves is acknowledged in the Crick Report as having contributed to the work of the Advisory Group on Citizenship (QCA 1998a: 83).

The belief that the government is keen to take up Hargreaves' agenda appears confirmed by the publication of the DEMOS text, *Learning Beyond the Classroom* (Bentley 1998), which reiterates Hargreaves' ideas in the context of education in the late 1990s. Although DEMOS is an independent think-tank, at the time he wrote the book, Bentley was not only an adviser to David Blunkett, MP, Secretary of State for Education and Employment, he was also a member of the Advisory Group on Citizenship (QCA 1998a:

5). Bentley proposes 'active, community-based learning' (Bentley 1998: 30) which would create responsible, independent learners (see Chapter 1). If adopted, the radical, and perhaps idealistic, proposals of Hargreaves and Bentley would require major changes not only to the curriculum but also to the organization of schools. At this stage it is difficult to believe that such radical changes will be made.

Nevertheless, the work of socio-linguists such as Gee, Lankshear, Mercer and others offers teachers the possibility of developing pupils' social literacy through participation, collaboration and negotiation; by making Discourses visible through exploring the underpinning values and beliefs. Whatever the subject, the role of classroom talk and, in particular, 'exploratory talk' in the classroom cannot be underestimated: 'It typifies language which embodies certain principles – of accountability, of clarity, of constructive criticism and receptiveness to well-argued proposals – which are highly valued in many societies' (Mercer 1995: 106). In key social institutions such as the law, government, administration, research in the sciences and arts, and business, language is used in sophisticated ways: for example, to interrogate the quality of the claims, hypotheses and proposals; to articulate understandings; to reach consensual agreement; and to make joint decisions. Mercer reminds us that it is in such language that 'reasoning is made visible' and 'knowledge is made accountable', not in any absolute terms, but in 'accord with the "ground rules" of the relevant discourse community' (Mercer 1995: 106).

Social literacy is fundamental to pupils' development as active citizens. If teachers are to develop pupils' social literacy, then the ground rules of exploratory talk in the classroom need to be made visible. These ground rules are: sharing relevant information; providing reasons for any assertions or opinions; asking for reasons where appropriate; reaching agreement; and accepting that the group, rather than any individual, was responsible for decisions and actions and ultimately for any ensuing success or failure (Mercer 1995: 108). By enabling pupils to *learn* these ground rules, rather than leaving them implicit and expecting pupils to *acquire* them, teachers will develop pupils' social literacy and promote their development as active citizens. The location of this learning within the current curriculum in England is discussed further in Chapter 4.

Conclusion

At the beginning of the twenty-first century the National Curriculum for England is founded upon 'traditional' beliefs about what should comprise the school curriculum: a menu of core and foundation 'academic' subjects. Despite the Statement of Values that accompanies the National Curriculum for England, there is no attempt to articulate the virtues which the study of the subjects themselves helps to form in young people. Although the

National Curriculum for England is supported by non-statutory guidance on citizenship and PSHE, it is insufficient only to inform pupils *about* aspects of citizenship: how parliament works, legal rights and so on. Such an approach to citizenship education is at the passive end of the continuum. The revised National Curriculum does not sufficiently acknowledge the complexities of developing social literacy. Simply engaging pupils in voluntary work within the community (cited by the Crick Report and the non-statutory guideline documents) will not of itself empower them. The values and beliefs embedded in communities, in facets of society, in the very aspects of citizenship about which pupils are being informed, need to be made visible, need to be reflected on and debated. Furthermore, in order to fully acknowledge the centrality of 'discourse' to 'active citizenship' (QCA 1998a: 14), the values and beliefs that underpin the educational discourse of the school need to be made visible to pupils, for the school is the social setting wherein they learn this educational discourse. Ultimately, the Discourse of citizenship education itself needs to be made visible to pupils so that they can critique its underpinning social values and beliefs in order that they may become active, transformed citizens. Such ideas are indeed challenging for curriculum developers and for teachers in school, for it would entail developing articulate, well-informed pupils who would be able to critique any curriculum on offer. Social literacy is both a prerequisite for and an essential requirement of citizenship education. It involves learning a series of social and linguistic skills and developing a social knowledge base from which to understand and interpret the range of social issues which citizens must address in their lives.

4 Social Content
The Whole Curriculum

Introduction

Discussing the content of a programme for social literacy leads into many areas of controversy. Previous chapters have touched on some of these: the extent to which there exists a consensus of values among educators, the competing methodologies employed to educate children socially, and the difficulty of measuring a child's development in these areas. What can most clearly be agreed, however, is that the current curriculum climate in education across the democratic world is one in which educating children in, through or for citizenship (Kerr 1999b) is a high priority. It is partly, but not wholly, within this context that social literacy has come to the fore. In many developed nations, social and civic education have had a high status for a number of years. Many Commonwealth countries, such as Canada, New Zealand and Australia, as well as Scandinavian nations such as Sweden (Kerr 1999b), have the development of the child in and through society as a foremost principle of education. In England, until recently, the curriculum was justified in part (NCC 1989) in terms of its ability to prepare pupils for 'adult life' but the word 'society' was notable by its absence in these principles. However, the introduction of Citizenship as a compulsory curriculum subject in secondary schools, and a non-statutory subject for primary schools, is perhaps a signal of a changing emphasis to the ethos of the curriculum.

In many ways, this new emphasis marks a return to some of the concerns of educators before the advent of the National Curriculum in 1989. A higher priority was given in all schools to social education, either in the guise of social studies, or through Personal and Social Education as a discrete subject. In primary schools, the social development of pupils has always been given a high priority, particularly in the early years of school life. However, despite the establishment of Citizenship Education, and Personal and Social Education as cross-curricular dimensions to the National Curriculum in 1991, and the requirement of schools to demonstrate that they are developing their pupils in spiritual, moral, social and cultural aspects of learning, academic subject-based learning has continued to dominate the school curriculum in the last decade. This has led, arguably, to the neglect of the values dimensions in education, in a climate where the more easily assessed aspects of children's learning have been given greater importance. Many schools have become concerned with delivering the content of the subject syllabi, under the constant pressure of OFSTED inspections and the publication of annual comparative performance tables. This concern has diverted attention from the more reflective aspects of children's learning, and it is through such reflection that children develop some of the types of thinking so crucial to the development of their social literacy. A further and more recent change, since the Dearing Review (DfEE 1995) of the curriculum, has been the downgrading, by omission from the review, of the cross-curricular dimensions. Concomitant to these changes in classroom priorities, a change in training priorities has occurred. Trainee teachers spend the vast majority of their time absorbing the content and recommended pedagogies of curriculum subjects, and have less time for reflection on the social effects and purposes of their teaching. This emphasis plays an important and valued part in raising levels of subject knowledge and application, but may not be allowing teachers to develop confidence in their ability to tackle the complex area of their pupils' social development.

The establishment of the National Forum for Values (SCAA 1996) marked the beginning of a return to an emphasis on the social purposes of education, albeit that many have been critical of the 'shared values' that its final report claimed to represent (see Chapter 2). There has since been a proliferation of reports from various curriculum advisory groups on: *Preparing Young People for Adult Life* (DfEE 1999c), *Citizenship and the Teaching of Democracy in Schools* (QCA 1998a) and *All Our Futures: Creativity, Culture and Education* (DfEE 1999a). This new curriculum climate could offer rich opportunities to schools and training institutions. With the renewed emphasis on values in the curriculum, there is a chance to reinvigorate the more philosophical aspects of learning and to place more emphasis on the development of children as autonomous thinkers. In the so-called 'information age' we are increasingly faced with a bewildering array of choices in society. According to Giddens (1994) the age of the expert is over, and we have to make decisions for ourselves. Developing the ability of children to be socially literate has arguably never been a more important curriculum priority.

The Current Curriculum Context in England

As previously indicated, the current context for developing social literacy is framed by the Early Learning Goals (QCA 1999a) and the National Curriculum (QCA 1999b); in the latter, this is through the values statements that introduce it, and the subject and non-statutory guidelines for Personal, Social and Health Education (PSHE) and Citizenship Education (QCA 1999b). The Early Learning Goals (QCA 1999a) have Personal, Social and

Emotional Development as the first area of learning that 'providers' should focus on. The goals listed (see below) promote children's development in intellectual, social and personal virtues. They should lay the foundations for later development, but are important in their own right, as there is over-whelming research that indicates how crucial this age phase is. It will be strongly argued later in this chapter, however, that insufficient curriculum attention is given to social learning at this age.

By the end of the foundation stage, most children will:

* continue to be interested, excited and motivated to learn;
* be confident to try new activities, initiate ideas and speak in a familiar group;
* maintain attention, concentrate, and sit quietly when appropriate;
* have a developing awareness of their own needs, views and feelings and be sensitive to the needs, views and feelings of others;
* have a developing respect for their own cultures and beliefs and those of other people;
* respond to significant experiences, showing a range of feelings when appropriate;
* form good relationships with adults and peers;
* work as part of a group or class, taking turns and sharing fairly, under-standing that there need to be agreed values and codes of behaviour for groups of people, including adults and children, to work together harmoniously;
* understand what is right, what is wrong, and why;
* dress and undress independently and manage their own personal hygiene;
* select and use activities and resources independently;
* consider the consequences of their words and actions for themselves and others;
* understand that people have different needs, views, cultures and beliefs, which need to be treated with respect;
* understand that they can expect others to treat their needs, views, cultures and beliefs with respect.

(QCA 1999a)

For children at Key Stages 1 and 2 (ages 5 to 11) in England, the context is provided by the National Curriculum (QCA 1999b). Personal autonomy is identified in the PSHE (QCA 1999c) guidelines as a key strand of social development. Pupils will learn to 'recognise their own worth, work well with others and become increasingly responsible for their own learning', under-standing how they are 'developing personally and socially, tackling many of the spiritual, moral, social and cultural issues that are a part of growing up'. They will learn about the major political and social institutions that frame their rights and responsibilities, and to 'understand and respect our common humanity, diversity and differences so that they can go on to form the effective, fulfilling relationships that are an essential part of life and learning'. Each Key Stage programme is then laid out under the following headings:

1 Developing confidence and responsibility and making the most of their abilities.
2 Preparing to play an active role as citizens.
3 Developing a healthy, safer lifestyle.
4 Developing good relationships and respecting the differences between people.

As previously mentioned, there are further curricular dimensions which impinge on the development of social literacy: in the National Curriculum (QCA 1999b), each academic subject is introduced with a preamble which explains the importance of the subject. These statements are highly value-laden, and various themes emerge from the emphases highlighted in each case. The values implicit in the justifications given for the subjects can be grouped under various headings: all carry messages about personal qualities which society values. Art, Music, Science, Design Technology and ICT are all said to contribute to the development of children as creative and imaginative thinkers, who can make informed judgements and aesthetic decisions. Other subjects are considered to develop the children as practical decision-makers, employing various skills: planning, questioning, evaluating, sifting through evidence, understanding and changing the world (Maths alone is given this privilege), arguing for their points of view, investigating and solving problems. These subjects are History, Art, Maths, Science, PE and Geography. Subjects can, it is said, develop reflective qualities also: Art, Geography, Music and Modern Foreign Languages are credited with developing appreciation and enjoyment, thinking about their place in the world, reflecting on a sense of fulfilment, and appreciating different countries' cultures, people and communities. Subjects can contribute to the development of: pupils' active involvement in shaping environments (Art); curiosity about the past (History); involvement in developing group identity (Music); competitive and positive attitudes to active, healthy, challenge-facing lives (PE); becoming both autonomous individuals, who are discriminating and informed users of products, and team members (Design Technology); curiosity about phenomena (Science); and initiative-showing independent learners, who present information responsibly.

The above sample from the curriculum documentation represents a rather curious 'shopping list' of desirable qualities, where the attribution of implicit values to particular subjects seems at times a little arbitrary. It is noticeable, too, that despite the presence of Citizenship and PSHE on the curriculum, the ability of the other subjects to develop social, collaborative or co-operative skills is limited, according to the accompanying notes, to PE, Music and Design Technology. Tellingly, the word 'collaborate' does not appear at all.

Other Curricular Contexts and Principles

Bottery (1990) suggested four foci of attention to assist teachers in the development of children as social and moral beings. These are:

- the fostering of the child's self-esteem;
- the heightening of the child's empathy;
- the furthering of co-operation between children;
- the promotion of rationality.

There are clear similarities between the four strands of the PSHE guidelines and Bottery's four foci, although these were intended originally as a framework for moral development.

A few further reflections on the nature of social literacy need to be added at this point. The goals outlined above in the guidelines for PSHE are uncontroversial and appropriate, but social literacy goes a little further than this. For, surely, it is as much in what someone does not do or say, as in what is done or said, that social competence is displayed. Plato, through the words of Glaucon in the *Republic* (Cottingham 1996), described the most just-seeming men as often being able to appear so while acting unjustly. Children too, if they are to become fully socially competent, must learn to subordinate their own thoughts and desires, when they perceive that the situation in which they are operating demands this. Using the definitions of Chapter 1, these children would be described as having a pragmatic and individualistic approach. Thus, avoiding making spiteful comments to other children, not swearing in front of adults and knowing when to offer help and kindness despite their selfish desires, will all mark out children as socially competent in the eyes of their peers and of adults. The socially literate individual knows what is acceptable and what is not in society, when to listen despite being uninterested in the speaker, and how to make people feel valued and at ease. These skills have been developed in large part through self-reflection on successes and failures in social interactions, through rational examination of the consequences of one's actions and words. They have also been developed alongside a growing knowledge of social mores, 'etiquette' and cultural codes. The responsibility of the school is to provide a whole-school context, and a curriculum context, within which this reflection can take place; where children can learn from their own actions and those of others. To develop the social virtues, as discussed in Chapter 2, reflection on action is required, if it is accepted that there is no true virtue without thought. There is also a need to recognize the multiple skills that children possess in this area of learning, in that they operate simultaneously in several different codes and communities. Juggling the rules of classroom, street, family and friends is no simple task. Yet, most obviously in their use of language, children from as young as 6 years old are able to switch from situations in which different vocabulary is used and allowed, without making serious errors. Arguably, it is the youngest children who should be our highest priority in developing social literacy.

Priorities: Early Years and Social Literacy

It is no longer a controversial assertion to make that the most important and formative stage of a child's social and moral development is during the years 0–6. Extensive research has been undertaken in the last twenty years into children's personal, social and emotional development at this stage. Dunn (1988) conducted longitudinal work with toddlers in their family settings, and found that siblings' moral interactions with 2-year-olds had significant impacts on their moral understanding as assessed seven months later. The very young child is intensely interested in the context of family relationships, and from the first few weeks of life can be seen initiating social contact and reciprocating it. Dunn also found that participation in the moral discourse of the family through explicit talk about rules and emotions also affected the development of moral understanding. In opposition to the ideas of Piaget, Fein (1984) found that children aged between 2 and 5 years old were able to transcend egocentricity in their play, if not in other areas of learning. Vygotsky (1978: 102) stated that 'in play a child always behaves beyond his average age'. Connolly and Doyle (1984) and Corsaro (1986) both investigated the types of play that children engaged in and the language that it generated. They found that children engaged in socio-dramatic play showed more social competences than those who did not, and that through such play, children were able to rehearse and resolve traumas of life, through issues such as lost/found, danger/rescue, and death/rebirth. Much of this work reshapes the ideas of Piaget (1932) and Kohlberg (1984) who suggesting that very young children have very little capacity for developing social understanding and competences, and therefore social literacy. Dunn in particular (1988) sees social understanding as an emergent property of relationships, not a 'within-child feature'. Gardner (1993: 51) states neatly that 'the theories of life, mind and self that have coalesced by school age originate in the constrained but playful interchanges of early infancy'. In England, for several decades now, the emphasis in elementary or infant education has been on this area, but alongside a focus on the development of reading, writing and arithmetic skills. Thus children in school when they are 5 years old will be coming into a world where formalized, text-based learning is valued very highly. For children aged 3 to 6 years old, the opportunities for spontaneous play are diminishing. Wide-ranging longitudinal research suggests however that a curriculum for the early years that is based on developing the child's ability to choose from a range of play-based and more formal activities can have dramatic consequences on their subsequent socialization. The best known of these studies is the Perry Pre-school Project, later known as High/Scope. Individuals were studied over a period of thirty years in the United States, many from disadvantaged backgrounds. Children were exposed to a structured, high-quality and well-resourced early years education, that encouraged them to make choices in their learning at a young age. The programme operated a system of 'plan, do and review', also known as 'mastery' learning (Sylva 1994). Children were given choices of activities to undertake during the day, and at each break in the day were asked to review what they had done. Follow-up investigations at intervals of several years revealed significant differences between the experiment group and controls in dependence on social security, possession of a criminal record, health, employment records, early pregnancy and other factors. Schweinhart and Weikart (1993) found that by the age of 27 the pre-school graduates had:

- higher monthly earnings (29 per cent vs 7 per cent earning $2,000 per month);
- a higher percentage of home-ownership (36 per cent vs 13 per cent);
- a higher level of schooling completed (71 per cent vs 54 per cent completing 12th grade or higher);
- a lower percentage receiving social services at some time in the past ten years (59 per cent vs 80 per cent);
- fewer arrests (7 per cent vs 35 per cent with five or more), including fewer arrests for crimes of drug taking or dealing (7 per cent vs 25 per cent).

It was calculated that the pre-school programme returned $7.16 for every $1 spent. The study suggests that developing the child's ability to make responsible choices through the curriculum is crucial at this early stage. A number of factors were key to the success of the programme: developmentally appropriate, child-initiated active learning; adult:child ratios of 1:8/10; systematic training for staff; attendance at the programme for two years for 3- and 4-year-olds; and weekly home visits by trained adults. The programme initiated what the Royal Society for the Arts 'Start Right' report described as a triangle of care, between child, school and home. A further study of the cohorts (Schweinhart *et al.* 1986) indicated that those children who had followed a more formal pattern of learning in pre-school often showed worse behaviour and attention to task in mid-adolescence.

In examining the curriculum frameworks for pre-school in other European and developed nations, a level of flexibility can be detected, which allows more time to be devoted exclusively to children's social needs. Although the percentage of GNP spent on education was lower in Sweden than in England in 1992, funding priorities allowed for a ratio of 4 children to 1 adult in the pre-school (2 to 5 years old) stage and for some in the transition year (5 to 6 years old) (Husen and Postlethwaite 1995). As in England, the curriculum at this stage is not firmly fixed, but there is a far greater emphasis on play, especially outdoors. Children spend at least an hour a day outside, regardless of the weather, and learn through their outdoor activities about the world around them. Daily walks through the community allow for discussion time and questions about the environment, traffic safety, community services, and help teach the children about their own safety. Games are played which show them what to do when they get lost – this for children as young as 2 years old. There is widespread social and political consensus in Sweden and other Scandinavian countries that this stage of a child's life is to be preserved from the pressures of formal learning, and is a long period of time within which to socialize them in learning to live and learn with others. In section 2.3 of the pre-school curriculum, entitled 'Influence of the child', the following quotation illustrates one of the key priorities for this phase: 'The social development of the child presupposes that in relation to their capacity, they are able to take responsibility for their own actions and for the environment in the pre-school' (Skolverket 1998: 13). In Germany (Colberg-Schrader and Oberhuemer 1993: 66) the aims of kindergarten education are clearly to provide children with an environment for social development, and 'to create a communicative milieu which enables the children to negotiate their contacts and conflicting interests, abilities necessary in later life'. The areas for development prescribed for the curriculum are (IRCA 1998):

- children's physical, mental, emotional and social abilities;
- a sense of responsibility;
- accustomizing children to daily routine;
- play and other activities.

In Spain (Aguado-Odina 1993), areas for development at 0–6 years old are: personal identity and independence, physical and social environment, and communication and expression. In addition, emphasis is laid (IRCA 1998) on 'language as a tool for the understanding of and involvement in one's own surroundings, the development of a positive and stable self-image and the acquisition of day-to-day habits as a way of acquiring personal independence'.

Finally, in New Zealand, the extract from the IRCA (1998) merits a full quotation, as exemplifying a holistic social approach to early years education:

> The curriculum guidelines for the early childhood curriculum in New Zealand are based on the following four foundation principles:

- empowerment: the early childhood curriculum should empower the child to learn and grow;
- family and community: the wider world of family and community should be an integral part of the early childhood curriculum;
- holistic development: the early childhood curriculum should reflect the holistic way children learn and grow;
- relationships: the early childhood curriculum should reflect the fact that children learn through responsive and reciprocal relationships with people, places and things;

and the following aims or strands (interwoven with the principles):

- well-being: the health and well-being of the child should be protected and nurtured;
- belonging: children and their families should feel a sense of belonging;
- contribution: opportunities for learning should be equitable and each child's contribution should be valid;
- communication: the languages and symbols of their own and other cultures should be promoted and protected;
- exploration: the child should learn through active exploration of the environment.

In England (QCA 1999a) a certain emphasis has been given to social and personal development, but by comparison the curriculum is extremely crowded with requirements for children's learning in other areas. Most notably, the pressure on early years' educators to develop children's reading abilities at this age has been argued by some to be counter-productive to their development as confident users of oral language, and to succeed generally in school in later life (Schweinhart *et al.* 1986; Dixon 1999; Stow 1996). It can be argued that the development of children's social literacy will not be receiving the start it needs, if children are in formal schooling from the age of 4.

Constraints

There are various factors which may constrain our attempts to define the areas of learning which social literacy should cover in its content. A lack of consensus on agreed values could be seen as one such factor. McLaughlin (1992) called for a debate which established what the agreed values in a pluralist society were, before any attempts were made to define curricula for citizenship. Such a debate has taken place since then, under the auspices of the National Forum for Values. The shortcomings of this Forum were discussed in Chapter 2. Beck (1998), however, suggests that it is precisely the contested nature of so many aspects of defining common public values which can be a significant learning point for children. McLaughlin also calls for schools to show commitment to the public values of democratic citizenship. These include (1995: 27) 'matters such as basic social morality, freedom of speech, ideals such as personal autonomy and the ... freedom of individuals to pursue their fuller conception of the good within a framework of justice through the distribution of "primary goods"'. Haste (1996) sketches an outline of a possible communitarian position on these issues. She argues that the value of personal autonomy is seen by communitarians as an unrealistic view of human behaviour and as damaging to the moral climate. The principles she proposes (for moral education, but equally applicable for social development) could in fact be contexts for developing social autonomy (1996: 53):

*   learning through language and social practice;
*   fostering social identity;
*   feeling engaged with and connected to others;
*   recognizing that institutions have multiple covert and overt agendas;
*   a self-conscious appreciation of the hermeneutic processes which generate meaning.

Curiously, given her opposition to personal autonomy, the last two in particular seem entirely compatible with goals of developing independence of thought and attitude in individuals. Objections are also raised to the centrality of 'personal autonomy' as a primary goal of education by Robertson (1997). He discusses whether such an ideal is appropriate for all children, and whether there are not more inclusive ways of defining 'being a person', which stress self-awareness rather than independence.

Other authors are more explicit in suggesting appropriate content for citizenship and social education. Osler (1999) is critical of the blandness of the citizenship proposals and in particular the lack of an explicit mention of racism. She suggests that the concept of political literacy needs to be expanded to give young people the skills to challenge racism and inequality. Klug and Spencer (1998) are critical of the restrictive nature of national frameworks for social and political education, and suggest that supranational frameworks already exist, such as the European Convention of Human Rights, which is now enshrined in English law.

It is clear from examining these various perspectives that a curriculum for social literacy which is too explicitly confined by content would be counterproductively contentious. The existing framework for PSHE and Citizenship clearly avoids being too prescriptive in content. In PSHE, the guidelines are designed to move children towards certain attitudes, towards themselves, society and the environment, and clearly borrows from the Values (SCAA 1996) statement in this respect. It does not closely prescribe behaviour. Nor should educating for social literacy prescribe that children should necessarily display behaviours or attitudes which are contentious. Primarily, it is concerned with educating them about society, and within society, to enable them to make informed choices as adults in contexts of social interaction. However, these choices are made by them as individuals, albeit within a social context, and having learned to make such choices in communities which have rules. As educators, we place great value on the development of children as academically critical. We cannot honestly do other than apply the same criterion to social development.

Another area of debate and possible constraint is around the teacher's role in social education. McLaughlin (1995) is against teacher neutrality and pluralism, suggesting that schools should be unequivocal in their commitment to the public values outlined above. Tate (1996) goes further and holds up schools, and by implication teachers, as being places in which 'pervasive moral relativism' should be tackled head-on. Haydon (1997) is dubious of both the morality and the putative effectiveness of teachers in transmitting values. He suggests that teachers should be aiming to develop virtues in their pupils, and to provide cognitive reflection on the actions that such virtues might lead them to employ. He is mindful here of the limited influence that schools may have, given that the majority of the child's time is spent away from school, and under other social influences. Pring (1984) talks, instead, of focusing on teacher neutrality, of the teacher assisting the pupil in moving from dependence on the authority of the teacher to the authority of evidence. Rowe (1999) is in favour of a social discourse model, in which teachers capitalize on social issues of concern to children, rather than imposing 'big issues' discussions and debates which have implicitly approved positions and arguments (Mercer 1995). His concern is to create a culture of discussion and debate, in which pupils learn the codes and principles of democratic discussion. Haste (1996) suggests that the role of the teacher is to provide contexts in which children reflect on social and linguistic practices, that lead them to understand their responsibility towards the community.

It could be proposed, however, that the teacher's role should be defined by drawing on a variety of approaches. If it is agreed that developing social literacy involves developing the child's knowledge of and abilities in social interaction, then the teacher must be involved in providing opportunities for reflection. Some of those interactions may develop the child socially, and therefore in relation to the community, but some may be in relation to purely personal choices and preferences. In reflecting on moral issues, children may be best served by discussing issues that directly concern them (Rowe 1999), rather than issues of 'topical' concern in the media. On commitment to public values, the ethos of the school may be more significant than the views of the teacher. In many cases, this may present the school as being at odds with democratic values (Griffith 1998), and older pupils will be aware of this. However, the teacher's own position on these public values will be evident in more than just their responses to certain debates and discussions, so the possibility of neutrality is virtually non-existent. Teachers ought to be in a position to play devil's advocate in such discussions in any case. Perhaps the most important aspect of the teacher's role is in developing a climate of reflection and meta-cognition. It is in developing the meta-language of debate and reflection that they can most effectively develop pupils in social literacy (Lankshear 1997). Research undertaken in the US (Gardner and Krechevsky 1993) has indicated multiple academic and social benefits to pupils of such an approach. Meadows (1993: 344) also speaks of the benefits of a Vygotskian approach, based on 'reflective abstraction of general principles of metacognition'.

Curriculum Opportunities

This section of the chapter has to begin with an admission – it cannot possibly do more than sketch opportunities for social literacy in schools. It is hoped that it can provide an idea of the main contexts for social literacy, and raise some of the issues that curriculum planners would need to consider when reviewing existing provision. As with Citizenship and PSHE (QCA 1999b), this is an area of children's learning that occurs in many differing aspects of a child's experience of school. But it is believed that social literacy is a fundamental aspect of children's development which goes further than the bounded domains of Citizenship, and PSHE, as defined by QCA (1999b). In reviewing the opportunities, Bottery's (1990) four foci of attention will be used:

- the fostering of the child's self-esteem;
- the heightening of the child's empathy;
- the furthering of co-operation between children;
- the promotion of rationality.

There are a number of aspects of children's schooling which provide opportunities for social development, and these will be dealt with in turn. Social literacy can be developed through learning in individual and discrete lessons and subjects, *within the curriculum*. It can also be developed by giving priority to key aspects of overall learning, *across the curriculum*. Finally, it is developed to a great extent by children's experiences *outside the curriculum*.

Within the Curriculum

A clearly defined curriculum exists within which educators in England must operate, and a useful starting point is to attempt to identify the opportunities for social development which are perceived to exist in the subjects of the Early Learning Goals (QCA 1999a) and the National Curriculum (QCA 1999b). Looking first at the subjects traditionally regarded as academic, it can be argued that, by learning in and about these subjects, children are being initiated into forms of knowledge and ways of thinking that society considers important and valuable. Thus the knowledge and cognition that they should develop will allow them to take part in important discourses in society. The development of literacy in English or language and literacy (Early Learning Goals), and numeracy in Mathematics are rightly considered central to providing children with the tools to take part in adult life. Arguably as important, and in practice somewhat sidelined in the present National Curriculum climate, is the area of Speaking and Listening. The Humanities, developing knowledge and understanding of the world (QCA 1999a), represent a long-established way of learning which engages children in fundamental investigations of human behaviour, motivation and action. Physical Education and physical development are fundamental to children developing safe and healthy attitudes to themselves and to their bodies, and initiate them into an area of human experience which is highly prized in twenty-first-century society. Creative development, through Art, Music and Dance, is 'fundamental to successful learning' (QCA 1999b). Einstein (quoted in DfEE 1999a) said 'Imagination is more important than knowledge'. Scientific and technological knowledge is vital to children growing into a social and economic world where the array of choices and information is bewildering. Adults, as consumers of products and news, are faced with conflicting opinions and research to support the benefits or disadvantages of particular products or processes and the science that lies behind them.

Many of these observations, or similar sentiments, can be found in the statements at the head of each subject section in the National Curriculum (1999). These have been examined earlier in the chapter, revealing an interesting list of valued human qualities which the subjects are designed to develop. A close look at the content of the curriculum in a few subjects also reveals interesting patterns.

The emphasis in all the subject outlines is on linear intellectual development. Indeed, this is the premise of the structure of the National Curriculum and its assessment framework, the attainment targets. How does this map onto Bottery's (1990) four foci of attention? It can be argued that the development of *rationality* is catered for in part by subject learning in the curriculum. There is explicit mention of how subjects provide contexts for critical thinking (Maths, Science, English), selection of information (DT, ICT, English, History, Science, Music, Art, PE), and evaluation (most subjects). It is only in Key Stage 4, however, that pupils are to make wider critical judgements intrinsic to the subjects themselves: in ICT, they 'reflect critically on the impact of ICT', and in Science they 'consider and evaluate the benefits and drawbacks of scientific and technological developments'. There is an implication here that profound reflective thinking is only a part of learning in mid-adolescence. Many would disagree (Schweinhart and

Weikart 1993; Gardner and Krechevsky 1993; Littledyke and Huxford 1998).

What is striking in the documentation, from the Early Learning Goals to the later Key Stages of the National Curriculum, is the absence of any mention of collaborative or *co-operative* learning. Occasionally, children are required to 'work with others' (PE, KS2, 7 and 11c); in Art at all Key Stages there is an emphasis on collaboration; and in ICT there is further mention of working with others. This is despite the statement in the Key Skills ('Working with others') section of the National Curriculum: 'All subjects provide opportunities for pupils to co-operate and work effectively with others in formal and informal settings.'

It is clearer that there are opportunities for the development of *empathy* in some subject areas. In Art, History and other subjects children are encouraged to look at the perspectives of others, from cultures and times other than their own – in English, at Key Stages 3 and 4, this is a separate section in the recommended reading: 'texts from different cultures and traditions'. In Design Technology, children at Key Stage 1 'develop, plan and communicate ideas from their own or others' needs'. Drama is given some prominence in English.

There are clearly aspects of constructivist (Littledyke and Huxford 1998) learning evident in the curriculum. But there is a striking lack of emphasis on the social and affective aspects of learning in all subjects, which theories of learning (Vygotsky, Bruner, Gardner *et al.*) stress as being so important. Subject teachers, and curriculum planners for the 3–11 age group, might choose to re-examine the Early Learning Goals and programmes of study in this light. The central tenet of this book is that meaning is constructed socially, through discussion, negotiation and reflection on social interaction. As adults, our successes and failures at work and at home are often couched in social terms. Gardner and Krechevsky state (1993: 121): 'Schools do provide some group activities, but students are usually judged by their individual work. By contrast, in many social and recreational settings, one's ability to communicate effectively and work productively with others is critical to a successful outcome.' It seems ironic that a curriculum and educational system which is designed to 'prepare pupils for adult life' (NCC 1989) should have at its core syllabi which make passing mention of the need for children to learn and construct meaning in all subjects collaboratively, as well as individually. In other national curricula, emphases are somewhat different: 'Learning should be based, not only on the interaction between adults and children, but also on what children learn from each other. The group of children should be regarded as an important and active part in development and learning' (Skolverket 1998: 8); 'The early childhood curriculum [in New Zealand] should reflect the fact that children learn through responsive and reciprocal relationships with people, places and things' (IRCA 1998).

It would be wrong to assume, however, that the current National Curriculum is solely to blame for this lack of emphasis on social learning. Galton *et al.* (1999) shows quite clearly that the prevalence of collaborative learning and levels of pupil–pupil interaction have remained fairly constant (and low) in primary classrooms since 1979, and Griffith (1998) refers to survey work undertaken with secondary pupils in 1993 which showed low levels of any kind of meaningful interaction in some classrooms.

It was suggested that social literacy is more clearly conceived by looking for learning opportunities in clusters of subjects. Gardner and Krechevsky (1993: 121) put it succinctly when they state: 'Intelligences do not ordinarily function in isolation, except in certain exceptional populations such as idiots savants.' This idea of clustered learning certainly tallies well with earlier ideas of PSHE from authors such as Pring (1984), who was somewhat sceptical of the value of itemizing children's development in all the separate subjects of the curriculum. He made a particular play on the value of the Humanities in developing social understanding. He emphasized the fact that the Humanities involve drawing on sources from all areas of human learning and understanding, in order to help students deliberate 'about values and in coming to understand themselves and other persons' (1984: 121). He also stressed the procedural values of the Humanities, and how humanistic learning could promote humanistic classrooms, involving active, critical learning where the authority of evidence held sway over the authority of the teacher. The separation of this area into different subjects was, he argued, particularly inimical to deliberative reflection of a broad nature. However, there is no doubt that each subject offers particularly rich opportunities for discussion and reflection on human ideas, attitudes and beliefs. For a more detailed discussion of how the History curriculum relates to this aspect of teaching and learning, see Stow (2000).

In the area of aesthetic and creative learning, Hoye (1998) argues strongly for the Arts, and Art in particular, as a rich context for social development. She suggests that children's art works are a combination of individual and social realities, as are those of adults, and that they acquire extra meaning in a social context. They allow children to 'share experience, to empathise and to learn' (1998: 150). A constructivist art-room, she suggests (1998: 158), would 'encourage pupil/pupil interaction, student initiated questions and co-operative learning, responsibility for learning, valuing of others' work, and the adoption of multiple frames or perspectives'. The influential report *All Our Futures* (DfEE 1999a) provides powerful arguments for the social and economic benefits of a greater curriculum stress on creative and cultural education. It argues for a conception of culture and creativity transcending the traditional boundaries or Arts subjects. It is through such education that teachers can develop the affective responses of pupils, developing 'emotional intelligence' (Goleman 1996) and 'inter- and intrapersonal intelligence' (Gardner 1984).

Literacy is a key factor in levels of pupils' self-esteem and confidence. Research has pointed to the importance of children being exposed to meaningful literate activities at an early age. English offers many opportunities for reflection on society through literature, the development of speaking and listening skills, and through writing. An area that has perhaps been neglected lately, certainly in primary schools, is media literacy. Children as young as 6 years old are being targeted by commercial enterprise, and with the expansion of the internet towards child-specific sites and companies, this will only increase. Young people have very high levels of media literacy, and schools should provide opportunities for critical reflection on the media, even at Key Stage 1. The delaying of such higher-order thinking in ICT, DT and Science until secondary education (QCA 1999d) is a mistake.

All curriculum subjects are rich with opportunities for social action, reflection and development. There is not room here to list all possible links. The key factor lies in the teacher's or curriculum planner's ability to identify and plan for those opportunities, and duck or adapt to perceived constraints.

Across the Curriculum

Many have argued that the death knell for meaningful learning in PSHE came with its relegation to a cross-curricular dimension (NCC 1990e), and its complete omission from the Dearing Review (DfEE 1995). Best's (1999) research questions the accuracy of such assumptions, although he is critical (1999: 12) of continued TTA and OFSTED focus on 'all but the most traditional concept of the core curriculum'. It is possible to argue, however, that it is by conceiving of social literacy as a fundamental aspect of all learning in school, and therefore of some cross-curricular conception of the area, that will allow it to gain most status. Anecdotal evidence has always pointed to the low status of PSHE as a secondary school subject, partly because of the way it is staffed in some schools, partly because of weaknesses in teaching styles employed (Learmonth 1997), and partly because of its low assessment status. We have argued that all learning is constructed socially, and therefore must argue that social literacy can be developed through *any* learning situation. This will include in the current English curriculum the subject of Citizenship. Rowe (1999) has argued against the 'big issues' approach to social and moral education, and has produced a popular and well-reviewed learning pack, *You, Me, Us* (Citizenship Foundation 1994), which focuses children on issues which may be more relevant to their daily lives. There is great value in this, and a strong tradition in primary schools of strategies such as Jenny Mosley's 'Circle Time', providing powerful contexts for children to reflect on social, moral, spiritual and cultural issues. But for children to develop their awareness of social issues, to develop the skills and attitudes appropriate to a variety of social interactions, and to develop their self-esteem across a range of learning situations, there must be a far broader commitment to social literacy in schools. Kelly states that 'true education in its entirety is a process of personal development' (Kelly and Edwards 1998: 164). Let us return to Bottery's (1990: 37) four foci. It has been argued that a greater emphasis needs to be placed on co-operative and collaborative learning in subjects, and this would need to be monitored across the curriculum. Opportunities for developing a sense of empathy have been identified, especially in the Arts and Humanities and through literature. Rationality can be developed through individual subject learning, but there is increasing evidence that a development of supra-rationality or meta-cognition is most influential in changing children's experiences of school. Novak and Gowin (1983) gave particular prominence to concept mapping and Vee diagrams as techniques for developing this, and the application of these, in particular with primary Science, has been explored (Stow 1997). Gardner and Krechevsky (1993) developed a programme called Practical Intelligence for School, or PIFS. This allied the theories of Multiple Intelligences (Gardner 1984) to Sternberg's (1985) Triarchic Intelligence, and identified three key areas of knowledge that pupils needed to succeed in school:

- one's own intellectual profile, learning styles and strategies;
- the structure and learning of academic tasks;
- the school as a complex social system.

They interviewed 6th- and 7th- grade students about these three areas, and found various limiting factors in the pupils' ability to articulate their knowledge. These factors have implications for all cross-curricular conceptions of learning. Gardner and Krechevsky (1993: 124) produced a 'hierarchical taxonomy of PIFS profiles, based on:

1   elaboration of responses;
2   awareness of strategies and resources;
3   sense of self as a learner'.

The limiting factors identified were: (1) lack of vocabulary, literal responses and an incrementalist idea of learning which suggested that everyone could do better if they tried more; and (2) helplessness, passivity and a lack of variety in learning strategies. All students, of high and low ability, had (1993: 126) a 'lack of understanding of skills and underlying reasoning processes which were similar in different areas'.

An 'infusion' curriculum was devised which gave opportunities for discrete learning skills instruction and learning skills instruction in specific domains. They found that it was in domain-specific contexts that the learning skills were most helpful to pupils. For a more detailed account of the project, see Gardner *et al.* (1998). A key factor in the programme was using home contexts to help students identify their strengths and weaknesses in learning strategies, and learning to use their strengths in school to help develop weaker areas of understanding. Bell (1998) has devised similar programmes for secondary students on work placements, and found an applicability in other areas of children's learning in primary and secondary schools. The High/Scope pre-school programme (Ball 1994) has already been shown to have significant effects on children's social development, by developing the children's choosing, planning and reviewing skills. In *Success Against the Odds* (NCE 1996), the use of day-books, personal tutoring and diaries was shown to have contributed to the success of a number of secondary and primary schools in areas of extreme social disadvantage.

Social literacy entails both the building of self-esteem and of the capacity for social responsibility. Skillen (1997) warns of the difficulty in building self-esteem in a curriculum context where pupils have little respect for the value of what they are learning: 'Esteem properly entails recognition of quality, and expressions of esteem are only felicitous when both the judge's perception and the activity are appreciated by the receiver.' He questions whether schools are the appropriate forum for the development of moral (and thus social) individuals, being hierarchical and rule-bound institutions that demand obedience over critical reflection.

Further than this commitment to developing children's meta-cognition, many argue that a rethinking of priorities in classroom activity is required if children's social development is really to be valued. Dixon (1999) surveyed materials designed to support PSHE and Citizenship in schools and found that 86 per cent of activities recommended featured discussion and debate. Yet only three out of the ten Key Stage 1 headteachers rated 'being articulate' as important. She refers to research which identified clear connections between inarticulacy and reading failure. Skillen (1997: 388) argues strongly that 'discussion and its habit take time; and not to give it time is to signal a disvaluing both of reflection and of conversation'. Discussion, he says (1997: 388), 'entails children learning to take themselves and others seriously in a pattern of give and take that is not only an echo of Piaget's examples of learning through play, but is a microcosm of freedom, justice and fellowship'. His final lament is the question 'Where is there space for this time on the school timetable?'

Galton *et al.*'s (1999) follow-up to the survey *Inside the Primary Classroom* highlighted an increase in teacher–pupil interaction and in pupil–pupil interaction in sheer volume, but identified that little of this interaction could be said to be developing higher-order thinking. The National Curriculum (QCA 1999b) introduces a new term to describe a familiar concept to curriculum planning, in the form of 'Key Skills'. These are aspects of children's learning which the curriculum as a whole should develop. This in itself is an encouraging recognition of the importance of learning to learn. There are six areas of key skills identified (QCA 1999b: 20): communication, application of number, information technology (is this a skill?), working with others, improving learning and performance, and thinking skills. However, teachers will have to be inventive to find opportunities for all these skills to be developed. As identified earlier, despite the assertion that 'all subjects provide opportunities for pupils to co-operate and work effectively with others', a marked absence of reference to social learning was identified in the curriculum as a whole. Specific opportunities for promoting reflective debate and discussion in a variety of group situations will have to be sought across the curriculum at all phases. In particular, the development of oral confidence in the early years is crucial to later social and academic success.

Outside the Curriculum

The two previous sections have outlined ways in which subjects and conceptions of learning which cross subject boundaries can help to develop social literacy, through providing opportunities for developing self-esteem, promoting co-operation and a sense of empathy, and through developing rationality and supra-rationality. Arguably, however, the most powerful influence of all on the child's developing social literacy is the institution itself. OFSTED (1995) accord a high priority to inspecting (a curious word for something invisible) school ethos, and the way that the school caters for the Spiritual, Moral, Social and Cultural development of its pupils. There are a number of key factors here to be discussed: the relationships between peers and between teachers and pupils; the nature of democracy in schools and the structures in place to enable participatory decision-making; the discipline structure within the school and the values implicit within rules; the nature of the curriculum experienced in school; and the structures in place for links with home and the community, and the values that these demonstrate. The school, as the first, and sometimes only, powerful experience of an ordered community, provides the child with a vivid microcosm of society. Lessons learned from their experiences within schools can be valuable, but they can also be damaging.

Pring argues (1984: 92–93) most forcefully that research into moral development by Piaget, Kohlberg and others points clearly to the social context in which this takes place as being highly influential:

> Young persons, as they grow older, are learning far more from the behaviour and attitudes of those around them than they are from formal instruction. ... Too authoritarian an approach to rules, to discipline, to relationships between teacher and pupil, or to the subject matter of the curriculum itself, will encourage a spirit of dependence, an

immaturity of outlook, and a failure to reach the kind of autonomy in which a young person can take responsibility for his or her own life.

Others (Osler 1999; Richardson 1998) warn against the dangers of institutional racism, or colour-blindness. Richardson (1998: 28) states that 'disaffection is frequently caused or exacerbated by the failure of the education system to provide an inclusive curriculum and pastoral system, and by inadequate cross-cultural skills in "assertive discipline" amongst teachers'. Osler (1999) remarks on the over-representation of black and other minority students among exclusions and evidence of glass ceilings for ethnic minority teachers during their careers as evidence that equality of opportunity is not guaranteed in schools. In theory, social literacy is a powerful tool for removing disadvantage, but if the practice as evident in the relationships in school does not match the rhetoric of policy then the tool will be substantially ineffective.

Faulkner (1997) refers to a wide range of research that examines the cultures of playgrounds. She discusses the nature of the playground as a site for social learning, and quotes from Kelly's study published in 1994 as stating that 'if left to their own devices, [children] often order their world into hierarchical patterns of domination, subordination and marginality'. All educators are anecdotally aware that it is during unsupervised play that incidents of explicit racism, prejudice and bullying occur. But these are often a reflection of policy and practice within the school building. The National Commission on Education report on effective schools in disadvantaged areas (NCE 1996) makes repeated reference to the value of all staff and children being involved in discussion about behaviour, and being involved in implementing change through school councils and other liaison bodies. In one case (p. 104), changes were made to the physical arrangements for play, allowing younger children to use a supervised space indoors, and a drinking fountain was resited to provide safer access. In another (p. 262), a secondary school provided spaces for children to do homework and use computers at break time, and encouraged staff to mix with pupils at lunch and coffee breaks. Faulkner (1997) also discusses the need to develop children's strategies for playing together, and for managing conflict and aggression in these situations. The importance of this arena for the development of social literacy cannot be understated. Reflection on incidents during unsupervised time should be built in to classroom discussion during PSHE and Citizenship lessons, and this discussion should form the basis for children's actions in future.

School rules form the child's first experience of an institutional justice system. It has already been suggested that a discipline policy and the way it is implemented is a crucial factor in developing children's social skills, and has a powerful effect on their self-esteem. The rules are the visible framework designed to guide and regulate children's behaviour. Once upon a time, obedience to school rules was seen explicitly as preparation for social obedience and passivity: Kant (1960) wrote: 'Children are sent to school not so much with the object of learning something but rather that they may become used to sitting still and doing exactly as they are told'; and Durkheim (1961) stated that it was by respecting school rules that the child learned to respect rules in general. Moral developmentalists such as Piaget and Kohlberg were critical of the notion of passive acceptance of rules. Partly in recognition of this, many schools now negotiate classroom and sometimes school-wide rules with the children, and phrase the rules in positive language. Children are offered 'choices' when they misbehave, to follow pathways which lead to praise and reward or censure and punishment. These policies often come under the heading of 'assertive discipline'. Skillen (1997) recognizes this as a legitimate attempt to deal with a wider problem, that is that schools are not influential enough to deal with moral education on their own. But he is critical of the morality of children learning to behave because it brings them prizes, or 'weekly raffle tickets'. Such policies are widely used, and widely praised by OFSTED and others (NCE 1996); but they also receive criticism (Richardson 1998). Pring (1984) warned of the dangers of excessive authoritarianism in this area; assertive discipline policies can be highly effective, but this is partly dependent on the way that rules and procedures have been devised and how they are implemented.

More fundamental than all of this, according to some, is the need for institutions to ask: 'Is the school a democratic structure?' Griffith (1998) argues strongly that if we are to initiate children into the values of democracy then the very structure of the school must appear to be democratic. The relationships in school, the model of the curriculum followed, the systems for decision-making and the teaching and learning strategies employed must give the child a sense of being a valued individual. All schools naturally use such phrases in their prospectuses, and attempt to nurture each individual in their care. But are the children really experiencing a democratic system when the curriculum they follow is largely non-negotiable to the teachers that teach them, let alone to themselves? Skillen (1997) suggests that the lack of opportunity for action and genuine interactivity (especially in the community) in school prejudices the opportunity for the development of real understandings of social communities and democracy. Its replacement by ever drier academic learning counteracts theories of many of the great moral philosophers, from Plato and Aristotle to Dewey. 'You learn to become something mainly by doing the things appropriate to being that something' (Skillen 1997: 387). In Sweden (Skolverket 1998: 8) the State decrees that schools must actively model democracy:

> It is not in itself sufficient that education imparts knowledge of fundamental democratic values. It must also be carried out using democratic working methods and prepare pupils for active participation in civic life.

> By participating in the planning and evaluation of their daily education, and exercising choices over courses, subjects, themes and activities, pupils will develop their ability to exercise influence and take responsibility.

In England at present, children have to choose between studying either History or Geography, and either Art or Music at Key Stage 4. Forcing children to choose between subjects which arguably focus most clearly on society is hardly the best way to promote social development and an understanding of democratic values (Bangs 1996). Decreasing opportunities for extra-curricular activities in schools is another factor which is inimical to children's social development, and to the exercising of choice.

Increasing interest in links between school and home (Holden 1999; Macbeth 1994; Bastiani 1996) can be seen as an encouraging sign of greater partnership and two-way accountability. It is vital, from the earliest stages of a child's education, that bridges are built between the social communities of home and school. Many structures have been introduced in England since 1989 which provide for more information about schools and their performance being available to parents and society at large. But many of these focus on academic performance to the exclusion of other factors. For many parents and children this one-sided emphasis will be fundamentally disaffecting. For schools to redress this imbalance, a variety of reporting and assessment structures need to be in place, which will allow children, parents and teachers to focus on personal and social development, and which show all concerned that this is a valued and important part of schooling. Successful initiatives in this area include: setting up education for parents in the child's school to boost parents' own confidence in their learning, and therefore their preparedness to support their child; providing on-site facilities for parents to come in informally to find out more about the school; staff in early years settings in particular meeting parents away from the school; information flow between school and home being supported by diaries, contact books and open evenings; and 'open-door' policies to reduce the fear of contacting teachers for some parents (NCE 1996). In some Swedish schools, staff are allocated families to liaise with throughout the period within which all children from that family are in school. At least one parent interview per year is devoted to allowing the parent to inform the teacher about the child at home, as opposed to being informed about progress at school.

A final factor can be the extent to which pupils are able to experience extra-curricular activities. These often offer rich opportunities for pupils to develop relationships outside their class unit, through a shared interest and common experiences. The extensive provision of these activities, including residential trips, sports clubs and other after-school events, has been shown (NCE 1996) to be a distinctive feature of effective schools, in particular with children from socially and economically disadvantaged backgrounds. In the OFSTED inspection handbook (OFSTED 1995), extra-curricular provision only rates a mention as an adjunct to the curriculum; it should surely be inspected as a key feature of the school's overall ethos, and as part of its contribution to the pupils' spiritual, moral, social and cultural development. Children's learning in these areas is often richer in a context which they have chosen as an area of personal interest.

Conclusion

This chapter has outlined the nature of opportunities for the development of social literacy. The context is provided in England by the National Curriculum, through separate subjects and cross-curricular key skills, and by the Early Learning Goals. It was stressed that the years 3–6 are particularly important in providing the basis for social literacy, and concern was expressed at the possible harm done by over-formalization of early learning. Social, educational and psychological research was referred to in support of this, indicating the dangers of developing 'learned helplessness' (Sylva 1994). A framework for the development of social literacy was proposed, using Bottery's (1990) four foci of attention. To this end, a strong case was made for more social learning in all areas of the curriculum and at all phases of education. The emphasis of official curriculum documentation was shown to be on linear intellectual development, largely to the exclusion of collabo-rative and co-operative learning, and this was questioned. Opportunities were identified in a number of aspects of school life, within, across and outside the curriculum. A key factor underlying all of these opportunities was said to be the ethos of the school, and the extent to which it allowed space for pupils to reflect frequently and in depth on their social interaction. A lack of time for discussion and debate was proposed as being particularly inimical to the development of social literacy.

None of the above is intended to question or undermine an emphasis in schools on the acquisition of basic skills for learning; indeed, the impor-tance of literacy and numeracy in assisting social development and combating social exclusion has been stressed. Nor should it imply an increased workload for schools. Schools have been focusing on this area of children's learning for many years. It is more a question of shifting emphases in teaching and learning objectives, and adjusting assessment cultures (see Chapter 6). This implies giving greater flexibility within the curriculum, rather than just the addition of new subjects. It also implies a reconceptual-ization of learning in certain areas of the curriculum. It calls for a return to clearer emphases on values in subject learning, to highlighting and actively providing for the cross-curricular links which make subject learning mean-ingful, and to an emphasis on pupils learning about their own thinking. Passive learners should not be at home in a true democracy. The acquisition of social literacy enables children to participate more fully in human society, by helping them to make autonomous, informed and moral choices. But they acquire this ability through critical reflection on their own social experiences, and that cannot be done through formal instruction. Finally, supported by arguments developed earlier in the book, this chapter calls for a wider agenda to be opened for discussion and debate. Recognition must be given more clearly to the role that society at large, including commerce, industry and the media, plays in developing children's social and moral attitudes and behaviour, a role which may sometimes hamper the work that schools are doing to lead children to social virtues. Raising levels of social literacy is a massive national undertaking, and it can only be effective if the whole of society is committed to the task.

5 Social Literacy and Service

Introduction

Over the last two centuries, the concept of service has informed the development of education aimed at the social development of pupils. Our discussion in Chapter 3 of the importance of Discourse in relation to versions of citizenship showed how citizenship education would vary in relation to the type of citizen an education system would wish to produce. Just as we identified active and passive versions of citizenship, it is also possible to identify different versions of service. The social dimensions of curricula aimed at developing service learning in pupils may also be located in the quadrants described in Figure 3.1. In brief, this chapter will show how the dominant discourses underpinning service learning have changed over time from palaeoconservative to libertarian and most recently to communitarian. Initially, the purposes of such education focused most on serving the needs of the nation in order to develop two related aspects of the life of a developing capitalist economy. The first purpose was the inculcation in pupils of habits and dispositions of thrift, prudence and industry in order to preserve social fabric. The second purpose was to equip future workers with the skills and dispositions, such as perseverance and humility, that would serve them well as workers. During the first half of the twentieth century, the construction of vocational and social education anchored in the workplace was premised on the notion of inculcating in pupils a desire to be of service to the nation, or society.

In the 1960s, however, there was the emergence of the notion that individual needs in relation to citizenship were equally important. Such concerns slowly shaped policy. In the 1980s vocational and social education was primarily driven by a desire to develop libertarian citizens (see Chapter 3), who would be able to operate successfully in a market economy. At the end of the 1990s, however, this approach gave way to a commitment to the development of the social aspects of the curriculum founded on community service. The Advisory Group on Citizenship chaired by Sir Bernard Crick discussed whether 'service learning or community involvement initiated by schools should be part of the new statutory Order for citizenship education', but it 'concluded not to ask for their statutory inclusion' (QCA 1998a: 25). Subsequently, in the preamble to the non-statutory guidelines for Personal, Social and Health Education (PSHE) and Citizenship at Key Stages 1 and 2 the authors state the importance of pupils finding out about 'their rights and duties as individuals and members of communities' (QCA 1999a: 136). Later in the chapter, we discuss the issue of whether service learning should be required or voluntary. A debate on this issue has taken place for the last ten years in the USA where service learning in the community has formed the basis of many programmes in schools and colleges (see, for example, Anderson 1998). Whether voluntary or required, it is clear that versions of service have underpinned curricula aimed at the social development of pupils for at least a century.

Why Service?

A central question when examining the development of service learning is 'Who benefits from community service?' In contemporary parlance the question becomes 'Which of the stakeholders benefit from pupils being engaged in community service?' – the State, society, industry, commerce, the school, the community, the individual? As shown in Chapter 3, the prevailing dominant educational discourse that underpins the context in which educational policy is constructed will determine the nature of any aspect of education. Depending upon how the question 'Who or what is served by service learning?' is answered, it is possible to construct very different and even diametrically opposed versions of service learning, from the instrumental, which serves the needs of the nation, to the intrinsic development of the virtue of altruism in the individual. Many reasons have been advanced for the inclusion of a service element in the curriculum that might be grouped into four broad areas:

- pupil need;
- national need;
- community/society need;
- individual need.

Pupil Need

The arguments comprising the first group are based upon a view of young people as deficient in some way, and the intention of curricula constructed on this premise is to 'improve' young people, most often pupils from the working class. Such arguments were most prevalent during the first fifty years of State education, but the vestiges of such beliefs may still be teased from the words of some contemporary commentators (see, for example, Patten 1992). An early illustration of such thinking can be seen in the statement made by Lord Shaftesbury in 1859. Clearly, it illustrates the preoccupations of those who thought about the education of working-class children, in this case girls. He declared that he would like to see 'every woman of the working classes have some knowledge of cookery, for ... I am certain that they are ten times more improvident and wasteful than the wealthiest in the land' (cited in Sharpe 1976: 13). A statement built, it seems, more on prejudice than on fact. Nevertheless, it does exemplify the belief that it should be the purpose of education to correct 'natural' deficiencies inherent in working-class children, by developing in girls particular virtues and dispositions, such as thrift and providence. (Chapter 2 discusses the nature of the virtues and dispositions that might be the focus of a curriculum concerned with the development of social literacy.) Such an approach became the very stuff of State education, particularly in relation to the education of girls. Earlier, poet and HMI Matthew Arnold, writing in *Culture and Anarchy* (1869: 105), warns that 'the working class which, raw and half developed, has long been hidden amidst poverty and squalor ... is now issuing from its hiding place to assert an Englishman's heaven born privilege of doing as he likes'. Arnold was not alone in expressing concern about the working class and the growth of organized labour movements. During the fifty-year period that spanned the turn of the twentieth century, there were repeated calls for curricula that would develop in pupils 'habits of regularity, "self discipline", obedience and trained effort' (Williams 1961: 62), which would correct a 'natural' absence of such virtues. In 1921 the Newbolt Report warns of the great problems faced by teachers in fighting against 'evil habits' of pupils which they have 'contracted in home and street. The teacher's struggle is thus not with ignorance but with a perverted power' (BoE 1921: paragraph 59). Here an official document displays a clear attitude to children from the working class, who in their culture of 'home and street' are believed to threaten established norms, not through ignorance, but by virtue of a 'perverted power'. However, views about the deficient nature of pupils were not only confined to the first half of the twentieth century. The Newsom Report *Half Our Future* (Ministry of Education 1963) is positive about practical subjects because they 'offer creative and civilising experiences beneficial to all pupils' (Ministry of Education 1963: 128). Similarly, much of the drive for the development of service learning during the 1980s in the USA came from a belief that many of the youth of America were alienated from the democratic processes of the country. Educators saw American youth as isolated and alienated from society and saw community service as a means of reconnecting them by helping them to gain a sense of belonging to a community (Kinsley 1991).

National Need

Closely allied to the first group of arguments, but perhaps far more pervasive, have been the arguments for curricula based upon the perceived future working lives of pupils. Pupils would need to develop attitudes, dispositions, skills and knowledge in order that they might also meet the future needs of the nation. Ultimately, such arguments are elitist and the version of service inherent in them is passive. Therefore, they might be located in the palaeoconservative quadrant of Figure 3.1. With the development of Victorian technology, the need for some minimum education among the burgeoning working class was recognized. Semi-skilled workers needed to read, write and, perhaps more importantly, to follow written instructions. Politicians, philanthropists, the church and policy-makers were beginning to recognize the benefits of the social dimension inherent in the 'appropriate' education of a growing mass labour force (Sharpe 1976: 12). Examples of the drive to develop attitudes, skills and dispositions in working-class boys and girls that would make them, as adults, of service to the nation may be found in the following official education documents: *Regulations for Secondary Schools* (BoE 1904); *Report on Questions Affecting Higher Elementary Schools* (BoE 1906); *Report of the Committee on Housecraft in Girls' Secondary Schools* (BoE 1911); and *Report of the Committee on Practical Work in Secondary Schools* (BoE 1913). The education of working-class boys was premised upon the need to develop skills, aptitudes and dispositions, such as perseverance, accuracy and industry, in preparation for their future working lives through 'Manual Instruction': the precursor of curricular subjects such as gardening, woodwork, metalwork and design technology. Halsey (1961: 394) sums up the limited aims of education at the time, which were to 'ensure discipline, and to obtain respect for private property and the social order, as well as to provide that kind of education which was indispensable in an expanding industrial and commercial nation'. In his speech in the House of Commons at the end of the First World War, Lloyd George argued that 'the most formidable institution we had to fight in Germany was not the arsenals of the Krupps or the yards in which they turned out submarines, but the schools of Germany. ... An educated man is a better worker, a more formidable warrior, and a better citizen' (cited in Davison 1997: 24). When the President of the Board of Education, H. A. L. Fisher, introduced to Parliament the Bill that was to become the 1918 Education Act, he stated:

> There is a growing sense, not only in England but through Europe, and I may say especially in France, that the industrial workers of the country are entitled to be considered primarily as citizens and as fit subjects for any reform of education from which they are capable of profiting. ... They do not want education only in order that they may become better technical workmen and earn higher wages, they do not want it in order that they may rise out of their own class, always a vulgar ambition, they

want it because they know that in the treasures of the mind they can find aid to good citizenship, a source of pure enjoyment and a refuge from the necessary hardships of life spent in the midst of clanging machinery in our hideous cities of toil.

(*Hansard* 10 August 1917)

Although Fisher's speech goes beyond citing the usual functional, utilitarian benefits to society from the education of the working class to the intrinsic pleasures of learning, the deterministic nature of the future lives of working-class children and the attitude displayed to social aspiration both clearly indicate the elitist nature of Fisher's thinking.

While it is perhaps tempting to believe that such attitudes to the benefits of service are locked firmly in the past, much of the drive that motivated the development of the National Curriculum in the late 1980s was premised upon the perceived needs of late-twentieth-century industrialization. As discussed in Chapter 1, the major emphasis in the National Curriculum was on core and foundation academic subjects, which were supported by cross-curricular themes and dimensions. Two of the key National Curriculum guidance documents in relation to the social development of pupils were: *Curriculum Guidance 4: Education for Economic and Industrial Understanding* (NCC 1990b) and *Curriculum Guidance 6: Careers Education and Guidance* (NCC 1990c).

The 'Foreword' of *Curriculum Guidance 4* by the Chair and Chief Executive of the National Curriculum Council, Duncan Graham, shows how strongly the educational philosophy of its authors can be located in the libertarian quarter of Figure 3.1. Graham (NCC 1990b) writes 'education for economic and industrial understanding is an essential part of every pupil's curriculum. It helps pupils understand the world in which they live and prepares them for life and work in a rapidly changing, economically competitive world.' The authors of the *Guidance* believe that such education prepares pupils 'for future economic roles: as producers, consumers and citizens in a democracy' and that it will 'help them to contribute to an industrialised, highly technological society' (NCC 1990b: 1) – sentiments similar to those expressed one hundred years earlier. The document is very clear that it is imperative for pupils to 'develop attitudes needed to participate responsibly in economic life' (NCC 1990b: 4). It continues, 'Education for enterprise means two things. First, it means developing the qualities needed to be an "enterprising person", such as the ability to tackle problems, take initiatives, persevere, be flexible, and work in teams. Secondly, and more specifically, it means taking part in small-scale businesses and community enterprise projects designed to develop these qualities' (NCC 1990b: 6). The foundation of all such 'community enterprise' is not service, but 'profit' (NCC 1990b: 44). The involvement by pupils in the Mini Enterprise in Schools Projects was underpinned by the aim to produce entrepreneurial citizens able to engage in the Thatcherite economic market place that they would encounter when they left school.

Community/Society Need

Unquestionably, few contemporary politicians, policy-makers or commentators would make an appeal to a notion of nationhood. Nevertheless, similar beliefs related to the social purposes of education and their importance to the social well-being of society underpin the New Labour government's development of educational policy. Chapter 3 shows that there is a clear government agenda for education premised on the belief that the perceived problems of society, such as marital breakdown, rising crime and the lack of a sense of community, might be best addressed by schools. Such beliefs, however, are far from new and may be discerned as a clear thread in the development of service-based curricula since the beginning of State education. The arguments put forward for the importance of the social dimension of the curriculum are founded on two assumptions. One assumption is the idea that poverty might be alleviated, or perhaps eliminated, through the development in working-class girls of the habits of thrift and careful housekeeping. The standard of living of the working class would rise if women learned to budget more effectively. It is interesting to note that the Report of the National Advisory Group on PSHE, *Preparing Young People for Adult Life*, includes reference to the importance of developing pupils' 'financial literacy' (DfEE 1999c: 24). The second assumption is a direct result of the Victorian ideal of the sexual division of labour. Dyhouse (1978: 301) discusses the Victorian concept of a woman's mission as 'spiritual and moral guardian of the home', which was premised on the argument that 'a good housewife provided a cosy home, and was ready with hot meals on the table when her husband returned from work. Home would then constitute rather more than a refuge from the business of the outside world – it would provide an antidote to the lure of the pubs or streets.' Politicians and educational policy-makers believed that schooling aimed at developing social virtues would establish the family as the prime cohesive force in society. Similar beliefs about the primacy of the family as a force of social cohesion underpinned much of the debate surrounding the repeal of Section 28 in the early months of the twenty-first century.

It is unsurprising then that throughout the twentieth century the curriculum offered to girls emphasized the development of dispositions or social virtues related to appearance, neatness, thrift, care and cleanliness in an effort to raise standards of working-class life. The *Report of the Consultative Committee on Differentiation of the Curriculum for Boys and Girls, Respectively* (BoE 1923), chaired by Hadow, discussed what its authors saw as the difference in the social function of boys and girls. It assumed that all children had to be educated with two ends in view: 'i) to earn their own living; ii) to be useful citizens'. However, the Report continues 'while girls have also to be prepared iii) to be the makers of homes' (BoE 1923: paragraph 94). The sentiment expressed in point (iii) is further reinforced in 1926 by the Hadow Report (BoE 1926) on *The Education of the Adolescent*, which focuses on the teaching of housewifery to working-class girls for the good of society. It proposed that girls 'should be shown that on efficient care and management of the home depend the health, happiness and prosperity of the nation' (BoE 1926: xviii).

The patterns of education aimed at developing working-class children for their future lives that were set up during the first thirty years of the twentieth century were dominant even after the Second World War. Indeed, they formed the basis of State education until its revision with the establishment of the National Curriculum in the Education Reform Act of 1988. The purpose of the 1944 Butler Education Act was to regenerate the country and provide an education system that would develop pupils to their fullest potential. The Act also made it the duty of all local authorities to contribute to the spiritual, moral, mental and physical development of the community. However, it could be seen that the establishment of a tripartite system of schooling comprising grammar, technical and modern schools was premised on beliefs about the development of aptitudes appropriate to future working lives and was one of the causes of underachievement of working-class children (Davison 2000: 248). Major educational reports focusing on the preparation of adolescents for their working lives displayed similar views to those expressed in the 1920s. However, the terms of reference of the Crowther Committee do signal a change in attitude. The Committee was charged with consideration of the education of boys and girls between the ages of 15 and 18 years 'in relation to the changing social and industrial needs of our society, and the needs of its individual citizens'. The inclusion of the needs of individuals as well as the needs of society in the terms of reference appears to indicate a shift in political thinking in relation to the social and vocational development of pupils. Nevertheless, the Report considers it 'sound educational policy to take account of *natural* interests' (our emphasis). The *natural* interests of a girl are defined as 'dress, personal appearance and problems in human relations' because 'the incentive for girls to equip themselves for marriage and home-making is genetic'. Therefore, the Report proposes that such concerns 'should be a central part of her education' (Ministry of Education 1959: 32). Clearly, the authors of the Report were not in agreement with John Stuart Mill, who had argued that 'calling distinctions in their social and intellectual situation "Nature" is preeminently a political act' (1909: 27). Four years after Crowther, the Newsom Report, *Half Our Future* (Ministry of Education 1963), on the education of children from 13 to 16 years old 'of less than average ability', avers that girls 'may need all the more the education that a good school can give in the wider aspects of home-making, and in the skills that will reduce the element of domestic drudgery' (Ministry of Education 1963: 135). It is aware of the dangers of an overemphasis on curriculum differentiation in relation to practical subjects. The Report states:

> We have not labelled crafts 'boys' or 'girls', although workshop crafts will be taken by boys and domestic crafts by girls. ... We welcome, however, the fact that some schools achieve sufficiently flexible organi-sation to allow boys to take cookery if they wish, and girls, handicraft or technical drawing; and where a school has vocationally-slanted courses related for example to catering or the clothing trades, the conventional divisions of boys' and girls' interests will clearly not apply.
>
> (Ministry of Education 1963: 131)

These are fine sentiments, but on the following page, in its discussion of the 'vocational relevance' of Art and related crafts, the Report states that 'Design, function, decoration, display and communication, have special significance for those who may one day work in shops, in commerce, in the dress and clothing and furnishing trades, in textiles, buildings and printing; and, not least, for the future housewife' (Ministry of Education 1963: 132).

Thirty-five years later, and six months after publication of the Crick Report, the Report by the National Advisory Group on Personal, Social and Health Education, *Preparing Young People for Adult Life* (DfEE 1999c), was published. In the 'Foreword' to the Report, Secretary of State for Education and Employment David Blunkett details the benefits of 'good PSHE'. These benefits include the opportunity 'to learn the value of family life, including marriage, good parenting and stable relationships'.

Individual Need

The Crowther Committee does signal a change in attitude. The Committee was charged with consideration of the education of boys and girls between the ages of 15 and 18 years 'in relation to the changing social and industrial needs of our society, and the needs of its individual citizens'. In order fully to fulfil the aims of the 1944 Education Act, the Report proposes that the school leaving age should be raised to 16 years and that the final year in the secondary modern school should be seen as a transition from school to the world of work. In relation to the curriculum for students in further educa-tion, the Report identifies four main curricular aims that enable young workers to find their way in the adult world, which include training for citi-zenship. Other aims relate to moral values, education for leisure and vocational education. Lawton (1973: 108) is critical of the Report because it 'failed to make any real link between the excellent early chapters on social change and the later chapters on curriculum. ... Despite the extensive use of the Report by sociologists to support arguments about equality of opportunity, from the point of view of curriculum it is a very conservative, unimaginative document.'

In terms of a development in pupils of a sense of community, the Newsom Report offers two areas of focus: internal and external. The Report promotes the positive aspects of service to the community of the school through 'work or activities specifically communal in nature – a mural for the dining room, a lectern for the hall, curtains for the stage ... providing refreshments for some social occasion' because 'the knowledge that they are contributing, and the public appreciation of their efforts, can strengthen morale of many of our boys and girls' (Ministry of Education 1963: 131). Two chapters, 'The School Community' and 'Going out in the World', recommend that schools should provide opportunities for 'developing group responsibilities' and 'community service projects' (Ministry of Education 1963: 71). Clearly, the Report has moved beyond a consideration only of vocational preparation in order to serve the needs of society, to the promotion of community service and the development of individual self-esteem. The chapter on 'Spiritual and Moral Development' acknowledges the difficulties faced by schools where the values underpinning the educational discourse may be at variance with pupils' primary Discourse (see Chapter 3 for a discussion of the importance of discourse in relation to social literacy). The Report notes that within the

difference of standard between the multiple worlds of which we are all citizens lies a limiting factor to what a school can do. Its influence may well be only temporary, having no carry-over, unless it succeeds in making clear to its members that the standards it sets, and often in large measure achieves, are just as relevant to the whole of life as to the part which is lived within its walls. There is no automatic transfer of values; boys and girls need to be convinced that what applies in school ought to apply to all human relations.

(Ministry of Education 1963: 53)

The Report contains four recommendations related to spiritual and moral development and each proposes the traditional benefits of well-structured Religious Education. Lawton (1973) notes a change of attitude in the Report to the social education of pupils. 'Here is a slight ideological shift, moving away from elitist notions to ideals of social justice and equality' (Lawton 1973: 109), which is in keeping with a general tendency for industrial societies to move away from an elitist view of society towards a more egalitarian view.

The National Curriculum documents *Curriculum Guidance 7: Environmental Education* (NCC 1990d), and *Curriculum Guidance 8: Education for Citizenship* (NCC 1990e) also show a growing concern with the benefits of service learning in relation to individual needs. The 'guiding principles' of environmental education include 'the common duty of main-taining, protecting and improving the quality of the environment' and 'the way in which each individual, by his own behaviour, particularly as a consumer, contributes to the protection of the environment' (NCC 1990d: 3). The purpose of such education is pupils' acquisition of the 'knowledge, values, attitudes, commitment and skills needed to protect and improve the environment' by encouraging pupils to examine and interpret the environment from a range of perspectives that include the 'aesthetic, ethical and spiritual' (NCC 1990d: 3). The personal and social skills listed in the document that can be developed through environmental education appear to be remarkably limited. The skills are 'working co-operatively with others, e.g. participating in group activities for the environment' and 'taking individual and group responsibility for the environment, e.g. for disposal of litter' (NCC 1990d: 6). Attitudes to be developed are appreciation, independence of thought, respect, tolerance and open-mindedness. Ultimately, the main focus of this document is an environmental education anchored in the core and foundation subjects of the National Curriculum. Perhaps because the 'NCC recognizes that environmental education is the subject of considerable debate' it states strongly that some issues are 'controversial and it is important that they are presented in a balanced way, which recognizes all points of view' (NCC 1990d: 1). Ultimately, the type of adult this document wishes to produce might be best described as knowledgeable but tolerant and, therefore, at the passive end of the citizenship continuum in Figure 3.1 (see p. 28). Lawton (1973) neatly sums up the inadequacy of such an approach to education for social awareness:

> It is not simply educating for toleration, it also involves knowing what are the limits of toleration and where it may be necessary to stand firmly on one's principles. All of this is quite impossible without a high level of understanding, not only of politics and economics but also of what values are, why value systems are similar in some respects and different in others, what principles are involved in making values-judgements, and so on.
>
> (Lawton 1973: 133)

A key feature of education for citizenship stated in *Curriculum Guidance 8* is 'to strengthen the bond between the individual and community' (NCC 1990e: 1). However, the document is 'not a blueprint or set of lesson plans' (NCC 1990e: 1). The curricular objectives of *Education for Citizenship* are knowledge, cross-curricular skills, attitudes, moral codes and values. Central to the first objective is development of knowledge and understanding of 'The nature of community' comprising: local and world-wide communities; how communities combine stability with change; the organization of communities and the importance of rules and laws; and how communities reconcile the needs of the individual with those of society (NCC 1990e: 3). Also included in this objective are 'Roles and relationships in a democratic society' and 'The nature and basis of duties, responsibilities and rights' including moral responsibility (NCC 1990e: 3). The promotion of positive attitudes is cited, including: independence of thought on social and moral issues; enterprise; persistence; sense of fair play; respect; a constructive interest in community affairs; concern for human rights. In its discussion of moral codes and values, the document goes beyond some of the hitherto simplistic representations of the development of personal moral codes. The document promotes the development of shared values 'such as concern for others, industry and effort, self-respect and self-discipline, as well as moral qualities such as honesty and truthfulness'. It also acknowledges that 'distinguishing between right and wrong is not always straightforward' because an 'individual's values, beliefs and moral codes change over time and are influenced by personal experience (e.g. of the family, friends, the media, school, religion) and the cultural background in which an individual is raised' (NCC 1990e: 4). If only implicitly, the document exemplifies the importance of knowledge and understanding of discourse to the development of social literacy discussed in Chapter 3. It proposes that pupils should be given opportunities to compare their own beliefs and values with others and to identify common ground; to examine evidence and opinion; to form conclusions; to discuss differences and resolve conflict; and to discuss and consider solutions to personal and social moral dilemmas. However, much of what is proposed in relation to Key Stages 1–4 follows the 'traditional' model of information gathering in core and foundation subjects and PSHE. Community service is to be undertaken by pupils through 'a community or business enterprise' that is evaluated in terms of 'costs and benefits' (NCC 1990e: 4). Sadly, the document appears to be a missed opportunity to develop social literacy effectively in schools.

What is Service Learning?

Currently, the term 'community service' is problematic. Indeed, it might be argued that it has an image problem. The 'short sharp shock' treatment to be dealt out by the proposed 'boot camps' of the late 1980s having failed, compulsory community service was introduced in place of a custodial sentence as a punishment for young offenders. There appears to be no recognition in recent National Curriculum documentation that in the minds of most young people living in the United Kingdom today, any attempt to engage them in community service will be seen as a punishment of some sort. Without a great deal of work by schools and educational policy-makers to reposition community service as a positive aspect of young people's lives, service learning is unlikely to become a successful facet of the curriculum on offer in schools.

Service Learning in the National Curriculum

The Report of the National Advisory Group on Personal, Social and Health Education, *Preparing Young People for Adult Life* (DfEE 1999c), proposes that schools should provide pupils with opportunities for them 'to play a positive part in the life of their school, neighbourhood and communities'. In a paragraph reflecting Bentley (1998), the Report notes that the learning environment goes beyond the school, because the school 'is part of the community and learning opportunities will be offered by the quality of the school's relationship with the wider community' (DfEE 1999c: 2). The Report identifies the roles of significant contributors to PSHE, including parents, schools, governors, pupils, FE colleges, health services and central government. From the community it cites such significant contributors as 'the people living in the locality, the shops, the services and amenities which serve them, the churches and other religious groups they belong to and other cultural and ethnic groups with which they identify' (DfEE 1999c: 19). Other local and national organizations, and civic and voluntary bodies are mentioned as providing support for personal and social development 'often in conjunction with businesses' (DfEE 1999c: 20). Although there is mention of pupils working to be of service to the school in its pages, nowhere does the Report exemplify the nature of service to, or in, the community. Therefore, any school beginning to develop a model of service learning in the community needs first to be clear about how it will construct its model.

Will the school develop a model based upon:

- the community *of* the school?
- the community *in* the school?

or

- the *school in* the community?

What will be the underlying purposes of service learning? Will the school attempt to develop in pupils understandings that will result from:

- learning *for* service?
- learning *about* service?

or

- learning *from* service?

If curriculum developers in school look to the National Curriculum for answers to these questions, what will they find? At the heart of the revised National Curriculum documents is the *Statement of Values by the National*

Forum for Values in Education and the Community (QCA 1999c and d). The statement uses the refrain 'On the basis of these values, we should' (QCA 1999c: 148). Although schools and teachers are assured that there is general agreement in society on these values, the 'we' of the statement is never identified. On the basis of these values it is the responsibility of schools to enable the development in pupils of the capacity to: 'understand and carry out our responsibilities as citizens'; 'refuse to support values or actions that may be harmful to individual communities'; 'promote participation in the democratic processes by all sectors of the community'; and to 'contribute to, as well as benefit from economic and cultural resources' (QCA 1999c: 147–149). Both *National Curriculum for England* documents (Key Stages 1 and 2 (QCA 1999c), Key Stages 3 and 4 (QCA 1999d)) are premised upon a statement of values, aims and purposes (see, for example, QCA 1999c: 10–12). In the preamble to the non-statutory guidelines for PSHE and Citizenship at Key Stages 1 and 2 the authors state the importance of pupils finding out about 'their rights and duties as individuals and members of communities' (QCA 1999c: 136). At Key Stage 1, opportunities for interaction with the wider community cited are 'meet and talk with people (for example, with outside visitors such as religious leaders, police officers, the school nurse)' (QCA 1999c: 138). While at Key Stage 2, the 'Breadth of Opportunities' include 'meet and talk with people (for example, people who contribute to society through environmental pressure groups or international aid organizations, people who work in the school and the neighbourhood, such as religious leaders, community police officers)' (QCA 1999c: 141). The model of service learning exemplified in the National Curriculum at Key Stages 1 and 2 is based upon *the community of the school* (school nurse), *the community in the school* (visits by significant community members) and focuses upon opportunities for *learning about service*. These opportunities are, of course, at the passive end of community involvement and, as such, are unlikely to promote the active citizenship the National Curriculum espouses.

At Key Stage 3 the opportunities cited are similar but indicate a shift towards more active community involvement: 'meet and work with people (for example, people who can give them reliable information about health and safety issues, such as school nurses)'. This, of course, could be a passive activity based on *the community of the school, learning about service*. The example continues with: 'develop relationships (for example, by working together in a range of groups and social settings ... by being responsible for a mini-enterprise scheme as part of a small group)' – *the community in the school, learning about service*; and 'participate (for example ... in an action research project designed to reduce crime and improve personal safety in their neighbourhood)' (QCA 1999d: 190). While such involvement is undoubtedly positive, with the possible exception of the action research project (see below), it does not promote actual community service in a real sense as the engagement is more likely to be *academic* rather than *experiential*. Only at Key Stage 4 are pupils recommended to participate 'in an initiative to improve their local community' – *learning from service*. Other recommendations refer to the traditional 'work experience and industry days' (QCA 1999d: 193) – *learning for service*? Despite the fact that the revised *National Curriculum for England* is predicated upon clearly articulated beliefs and values, much of what is proposed in relation to community service is consistent with 'traditional' approaches to personal, social and vocational development. The only mention of 'community-based activities' in the programmes of study for Citizenship at Key Stages 3 and 4 is the phrase, which is identical in each Key Stage, 'negotiate, decide and take part responsibly in both school and community-based activities' (QCA 1999d: 184–186). On close inspection, however, this phrase is premised upon models of *the community of the school, the school in the community* as well as *learning from service*. From this brief analysis, it would appear that the dominant model of proposed service learning in the National Curriculum, with the possible exception of some activities in Key Stage 4, is passive rather than active. In the main, community service is constructed upon academic curricular experiences arising from models of *the community of the school, the community in the school*, which will promote *learning about service* rather than *learning from service*.

Effective Service Learning

Service learning should provide pupils with *educational* experiences which enable them to learn and to develop through *active* participation in thoroughly planned service experiences that meet actual community needs that have been identified by pupils and other members of the community. We highlight the importance of 'educational experiences' as not all community experience is necessarily educational, nor of the type that we would advocate as promoting social literacy. Unplanned, unco-ordinated voluntary involvement might leave pupils with a 'warm glow' of satisfaction, but perhaps little else of lasting value. Conversely, we would not regard highly organized and tightly structured 'work experience' as community service of the kind we advocate, for reasons discussed in the previous section.

Service learning experiences will be co-ordinated collaboratively by members of the community and the school. Effective service learning has four key components. These components are:

- preparation;
- service;
- reflection;
- recognition.

Effective service learning is integrated into the curriculum and offers structured time for pupils to discuss, think and write about what they did during the service activity. Such experiences should provide pupils with opportunities to use and explore developing knowledge, skills and understandings in real-life situations within the context of their own communities. In this way the experiences enhance what is taught in school by extending and supporting pupil learning beyond the classroom and into the community. Such learning is premised upon *learning from service* based on a model of *the school in the community*. Sadly, as we have shown above, it is precisely this version of service learning that is least represented in National Curriculum documentation.

Preparation

Community service projects may originate in a number of ways. Pupils conducting research on their community may identify community needs. This community might be the school itself, but such projects would carry the caveat above about the dangers of a model that focuses solely on the *community of the school*. Pupils might identify needs of the wider community in which the school is placed, either individually, jointly or in collaboration with members of that community. It needs little reflection to appreciate that teacher-initiated, focused and directed community projects are likely to reap fewest benefits. When pupils are engaging on a collaborative action research project, they will not only identify community needs, but they will also have to prioritize in order to identify areas of greatest need and make realistic judgements about the feasibility of their meeting those needs. At the same time, teachers will need to identify opportunities for learning within any proposed project: How does the project relate to other curriculum areas? What might pupils need to know, understand or be able to do before the project? What might they need to be taught before the service learning experience? What might pupils know, understand or be able to do after the project? What will they learn from the experience? How will this be logged, recorded, presented, assessed? What opportunities will the service experience provide for oracy, literacy, numeracy, research and problem solving? What affective outcomes might be reasonably expected – self-esteem, virtues, dispositions, habits, beliefs and attitudes? Although this list of questions might begin to appear lengthy and, perhaps, a little daunting, it is in reality no different from preparation for any other teaching and learning experience. Central to preparation for service learning is the articulation of the points raised in this paragraph.

Service

Aldous Huxley observed that experience does not happen to people; rather, it is what people do with what has happened to them. Therefore, community service of itself need not be a learning, or even edifying, experience – as the figures for recidivism among the recipients of punitive community service perhaps testify. Learning, the development of 'knowledge, understandings and beliefs is a synthesis of experiences' (Arthur *et al.* 1997: 77–78). The process of synthesizing enables pupils to focus, probe and test, and to begin to make sense of emergent attitudes, beliefs and understandings of themselves, their peers and the community. 'Experiences' as described here will not only take the form of direct involvement, but also they may also result from reading, writing or discussion with peers, teachers, community members or others. Pupils, therefore, need to be provided with opportunities for this range of experiences during service and, most importantly, they need to be provided with a means to record and document service. Pupils need to be supported in maintaining journals in which they record events, concerns, fears, pleasures, insights, doubts and critical questions relating to incidents, to people and indeed to themselves.

Reflection

Arguably, for community service experience to be worthwhile, pupils need to see the connection between service and learning. The experience needs to be 'made visible' to them. Data collected in service experience journals, logs, and so on, will enable service learning experiences to become 'texts' that may be studied by an individual pupil, groups of pupils and others engaged in the project. Clearly, experiential learning of which community service is a type has its roots in the writings of John Dewey, the most relevant to our discussion being *How We Think* (1933) and *Experience and Education* (1938). However, for Dewey, experience *per se* was not necessarily educative:

> The belief that all genuine education comes about through experience does not mean that all experiences are genuinely or equally educative. Experience and education cannot be directly equated to each other. For some experiences are mis-educative. Any experience is mis-educative that has the effect of arresting or distorting the growth of further experience. An experience may be such as to engender callousness; it may produce lack of sensitivity and responsiveness. Then the possibilities of having richer experience in the future are restricted.
>
> (Dewey 1938: 25)

Dewey's comments are a salutary reminder that community learning experience is not unproblematic. In order for experience to become educative, an individual needs to engage in 'reflective thinking', which Dewey defines as 'active, persistent and careful consideration of any belief or supposed form of knowledge in the light of grounds that support it and the further conclusions to which it tends' (Dewey 1933: 9). Through engaging in reflective thinking practices, pupils will be enabled to begin to see and understand things about themselves, their peers, their school, their community and, ultimately, about the society in which they live. In their early discussions/ writings, it is quite likely that teachers will see pupils being what they believe to be more *descriptive* rather than *reflective*. However, we believe that this fact should not surprise us, nor does it invalidate the activity; for it is in the initial stages, in such *articulation* or *description* of some aspect of the service learning experience, which may seem blindingly obvious to an adult, that learning and development takes place. Such description in these early stages can for the first time make visible the values, beliefs and attitudes present in the community. McIntyre (1993) identifies three levels of reflection: the *technical* level – concerned with the attainment of goals; the *practical* level – concerned with the 'assumptions, predispositions, values and consequences with which actions are linked'; and the *critical* or *emancipatory* level – where concern ranges to wider social, political and ethical issues that include 'the institutional and societal forces which may constrain the individual's freedom of action or limit the efficacy of his or her actions' (McIntyre 1993: 44). We would argue that pupils should be encouraged and supported in engaging in all levels of reflection. The work of Mercer described in Chapter 3 in relation to the importance of discourse in the development of social literacy offers an appropriate pedagogy.

What are the purposes of reflection? How will reflecting enable the social development of pupils? The following list (adapted from Frost (1993: 140) is by no means exhaustive, but it helps to provide answers to these questions. Reflection enables pupils to:

- assess his or her own knowledge, understandings and skills and to improve them;
- evaluate the approach to their community service project in terms of its appropriateness;
- comprehend and, where appropriate, question their own assumptions and preconceptions and those embedded in aspects of the community/society they encounter;
- continue to examine and clarify their personal values and beliefs;
- continue to examine and clarify the values and beliefs they encounter in the community;
- theorize about the context of their service learning – that is, to try to develop explanations about aspects of the community;
- examine the social and political dimensions of the issues that arise in their reflection on community service and critique the discourses in which they are located.

Recognition

Finally, it is important that there is recognition not only of service, but also of the learning that has taken place. While the first may involve a public or community manifestation of recognition, or celebration of a successful project – a plaque, a newspaper report, a ceremony of some kind – the second may involve a more personal dialogue between pupil and teacher, groups of pupils, or pupils and mentors. The second form of recognition may also involve community members, parents, siblings, and so on, in order that the school is recognized as a fully active member of the community. Pupils should be encouraged to develop a portfolio of community service, or record of community involvement, which might be used for assessment (see Chapter 6) as appropriate, but might also be used as evidence for further work – voluntary, or paid on leaving school – as a tangible manifestation of the qualities of an individual pupil.

The processes above provide a useful starting point for beginning to construct an active version of community service arising from a model of *the school in the community* that will promote *learning from service*.

What are the Benefits of Service Learning?

The essence of the benefits of effective service learning is mutuality. Instead of having a focus of primarily meeting the needs of just one of the 'stake-holders' in community service, effective service learning of the type described above has benefits for each participant: the pupil, the school and the community.

The Pupil

Unquestionably, the benefits to pupils are related to their academic, intellectual, personal and social growth and development. Engagement in effective service learning of the type described above will develop oracy, numeracy and literacy skills. It will involve them in higher-order thinking skills such as problem-solving and critical thinking. Not only will motivation to learn be increased, but also learning skills themselves, such as enquiry, observation and application, will be enhanced. Most importantly the pupils' capacities in relation to insight, judgement and understanding will be developed. In positive service learning, pupils' self-esteem, personal efficacy and sense of responsibility will be enhanced. Opportunities for moral development and the development of virtues and dispositions (see Chapter 2) will arise as pupils take on new roles, identities, challenges and interests and work collaboratively for the benefit of others. They will develop an increased sense of social responsibility and concern for others. Political and civic knowledge and understandings will also be developed. Ultimately, pupils will develop their appreciation of, and ability to relate to, a diverse range of situations with people from a variety of social backgrounds.

The School

The benefits of effective service learning to schools are equally important. If schools are to embark on another curriculum innovation as well as coping with another revision of the National Curriculum, what benefits might they expect? Effective service learning encourages pupils to play a more active part in their schooling and to take more responsibility for their own learning. Teachers themselves will find that they are acting more as mentors or facilitators for pupils. Increased pupil motivation and co-operative learning structures enhance the quality of work produced and the quality of classroom relationships. Teachers will become reflective practitioners engaged in curriculum enquiry and development. There will be increased benefits as a result of collaborative decision-making among school governors and managers, teachers, parents, pupils and members of the community. Effective community service will not only enhance the ethos of the school, it is also likely to mean that the school will have access to community resources, both material and human, to support teaching and learning (see Chapter 6).

The Community

The benefits to the community can arise from the provision of service to meet real human, educational, social, health or environmental needs. Schools – teachers, pupils and others – can serve as action researchers and resources in problem-solving and community development. Positive school and community partnerships empower not only pupils and schools, they also empower communities through joint planning, negotiation and resolution of community problems. Pupils are members of the community, and as a result of active and effective service learning experiences, they will become positive and effective members of the community as pupils and later as adults.

Required or Voluntary Service Learning?

As we noted in the introduction to this chapter, the Advisory Group on Citizenship discussed whether 'service learning or community involvement initiated by schools should be part of the new statutory Order for citizenship education', but it 'concluded not to ask for their statutory inclusion' (QCA 1998a: 25). The Committee reached this decision, not because they took account of any research evidence from the USA or elsewhere, but for far more pragmatic reasons – 'mainly from fear of overburdening schools and teachers' (QCA 1998a: 25). While we understand the Committee being rightly mindful of the dangers of innovation overload in schools, we believe the decision not to make service learning a statutory part of the National Curriculum for England is mistaken. Certainly, research in the USA suggests the importance of student autonomy in internalizing values and attitudes based on experience (see, for example, Anderson 1998; Deci 1995). An act of voluntary service is more likely to inculcate and develop altruism, philanthropy, self-reliance and personal social virtues. Hence, service learning would be promoted as an option and entitlement for all students at every academic level in all academic institutions. Pupils would choose to participate because attractive opportunities are available in the community. Of course, this approach places great emphasis upon the institution and the teachers within it to make the options available enticing enough that the pupils will choose to take part in community service – even the most reluctant. Despite the Crick Committee's assertion, we believe that a voluntary approach to community service is more likely to increase the workload on schools and teachers, not reduce it.

Statutory service learning aims to integrate service into the curriculum in the hope of making social responsibility part of the core curriculum on offer. Opportunities for reflection, support for pupil autonomy and opportunities for collaboration with peers, teachers, mentors and members of the community are all woven into the fabric of the life of the school so that *the school in the community* and *the community in the school* become inseparable, indistinguishable. Statutory service learning has the advantage of reaching all pupils and, therefore, has the potential to be transformative (Barber 1991, 1992). There is a tension because voluntary social activity cannot be coerced. However, we can speak of an education in service, or education-based service. Education cannot be left entirely to voluntary or discretionary response on the part of the child. Already we require pupils to become literate and numerate, because we believe these capacities will empower them in life. It is the nature of teaching that it exercises some coercion in the name of liberation. Social responsibility is too important to be left to extra-curricular activity. As we discussed above, the social dimension of the curriculum must be about acting and doing in real contexts – *learning from service* – not simply a cognitive activity – *learning about service*. Well-implemented service learning, just like any other well-implemented curricular activity, will actively involve, engage and empower pupils. Engagement in relevant service meeting real community needs that have been identified by pupils will make any concerns over potential charges of coercion redundant. The question of required or voluntary community involvement is to be kept under review by the Commission on Citizenship Education proposed by the Crick Committee. We hope that it will come to see the benefits of and to promote service learning as a statutory requirement of the National Curriculum.

Conclusion

The work of various Committees and Forums in recent years has produced the latest version of the National Curriculum for England that has the potential for significantly changing the ways school work in relation to the social development of their pupils. The curricula for PSHE, Citizenship and the so-called 'academic' core and foundation subjects offer the potential for the development of skills, knowledge, understanding, beliefs, attitudes, values, virtues and dispositions to an extent which has been unparalleled hitherto. Effective service learning offers a wealth of benefits to pupils, schools and communities. Statutory community service based on a dynamic model of *the school in the community* will promote *learning from service* that will empower pupils and make them the committed active citizens the government envisages. There is an African proverb that states 'It takes a whole village to educate a child'. Effective service learning offers the opportunity of making this assertion a reality in a twenty-first-century post-industrial context.

6   Assessing Social Literacy

Introduction

In Chapter 4, we discussed the nature of learning social literacy, and it was argued that it was something that was difficult to tie down to particular curriculum boundaries. Elements of the current curriculum guidelines for Personal, Social and Health Education (PSHE) and Citizenship (QCA 1999b) were said to contribute to pupils' development in social literacy, but opportunities for this development were also identified in all aspects of school life. It was argued that children's learning in this area did not follow a simple linear progression, despite the emphasis given to linear development in the National Curriculum. One of the inherent dangers in having a key area of children's learning which is not strictly defined is that it may be regarded as unassessable. In the context of PSHE, previous attempts were made (APU 1980) to establish an assessment framework, and subsequently abandoned, as the area was felt to be too contentious. A key text in this area (Inman *et al.* 1998) raises the question in its title: is assessing personal and social development attempting to 'measure the unmeasurable'? Bottery (1990) stated of moral education that 'such a rich, diverse and subtle field does not lend itself easily to evaluation' and that 'the ability to deal rationally with a host of difficult and complex issues in one area ... is not something which can be readily recorded on a developmental six point scale' (1990: 122). In the current curriculum climate, however, it must be questioned whether it is possible *not* to assess social development, if it is to be accorded any real status in schools. The establishment of PSHE/Citizenship as a curriculum subject (QCA 1999b) suggests that it is being given a higher status, and it is likely that forms of assessment will follow. A further contention will be the purpose of such assessment. Will it be another instrument to measure school improvement and provide evidence for public accountability of schools, or will it be a way of recognizing, rewarding and developing individual pupils' interpersonal achievements? Inman *et al.* (1998) propose that the very nature of learning in PSHE, and its focus on individual development, mitigates against any possibility of quantitative measurements for the purpose of comparing schools. In any case, qualitative comparative data is arguably available to the public in this area in the form of OFSTED reports on schools, which contain comment on the school's success in promoting pupils' spiritual, moral, social and cultural development (OFSTED 1995).

It will be argued strongly in this chapter that devising an assessment framework for pupils' development in social literacy provides rich opportunities for using formative assessment models, in which learning and assessment are genuinely integrated. A key strand of social literacy is the development of self-reflection and awareness, and thus self-assessment will form a crucial part of learning (Krechevsky and Seidel 1998). The model that will be proposed can therefore provide a form of assessment which has each individual at its centre, which allows for 'regression and development' (Parziale and Fischer 1998) rather than a linear progression, and which genuinely promotes the development of learning and autonomy by requiring pupils to claim 'competences' which are ipsatively referenced. The complexity of the pupil's development in social literacy implies that evidence of that development must be drawn from all aspects of the child's life; the assessment should encourage the child to perceive that learning and development is recognized in areas not traditionally given status in school-based assessment.

The first half of the chapter will contain a discussion of some of the issues which lead to this conclusion, and an outline of the model of assessment proposed. In the second half of the chapter, the strands of the model will be explained, and in each case issues will be discussed, possible foci and methods proposed and types of assessment outlined. Finally, the implications for schools and education as a whole will be drawn out. Recognizing that practice in the assessment and recording of personal achievement is already a strong feature of many secondary schools, the emphasis in the chapter will be on the early years (3–11) of education. However, general principles will also apply to secondary and tertiary education.

The Curriculum Context

As outlined in Chapter 4, it is important to recognize the existing curriculum framework for social development as a starting point for discussing issues in social literacy. This is no less important in the context of assessment. The Early Learning Goals (QCA 1999a) and the National Curriculum (QCA 1999b) set out a group of behavioural and cognitive goals in the areas of personal, social, health and emotional development and education, for children at the foundation stage, and at Key Stages 1 and 2. At Key Stages 3 and 4, Citizenship is also conceived as a list of 'tightly defined learning outcomes' (QCA 1998a: 5.6.2). However, it is interesting to note, in the same paragraph of the Crick Report, that the purposes for this conception are fairly clear:

These provide a fair and rigorous basis for assessment, reporting and inspection, both internal and external. They enable assessment by teachers of pupils' progress and progression in their citizenship learning. They also provide: a) the means for schools to report pupil progress in citizenship education to parents via the annual report on that child; b) the means to outline to parents collectively the schools approach to citizenship education through the annual school governor's report; c) the means to measure the standards and objectivity of citizenship education within and across schools; and d) information to OFSTED inspectors to assist them in making judgments on the quality of citizenship education in a school and the progress that pupils make.

(QCA 1998a: 5.6.2)

The anomaly of a curriculum subject designed to promote the development of autonomous, critical and self-confident citizens but which has no reference to the development of pupils' learning in its proposed rationale for assessment is striking indeed. But this anomaly highlights the potential dangers of PSHE and Citizenship (and therefore many aspects of social literacy) being assessed in future through pencil and paper 'civics' exams. The ideological non-sequitur that this represents has been referred to, but can be expanded on. For, surely, any curriculum initiative designed to promote individual and social development, or 'combat social exclusion' to use a popular phrase, cannot be measured quantitatively and summatively through examinations. Pupils cannot be classified as 'failures' in personal development without this stigmatizing the very pupils that such initiatives are designed to assist. Robertson (1997) is critical of the idea of a linear progression towards rational autonomy being a 'good' for all pupils, in that such a notion is specifically disadvantageous towards pupils with learning difficulties, some of which may be behavioural and emotional. He points to other definitions of what it means to be a person, such as Freire's idea of being 'one who can be part of a relationship with others who are sympathetic', or Harris's definition – 'being aware of itself as an independent being, existent over time and able to make sense of that awareness' (Robertson 1997: 302). In this light, best fit or numbered level descriptions of personal and social development, such as those produced by QCA (1998b), are surely counter-productive to the purposes of highlighting this area of child development. If the purpose of such measures is to give personal and social development curriculum status, or to provide accountability, then there may be other ways of achieving these ends. But, in discussing an area of learning devoted to individual development, such considerations deserve to be postponed, until the appropriate model of assessment has been devised. The key skills of the National Curriculum (QCA 1999b) are more focused on areas of concern to social literacy, but it was indicated in Chapter 4 that the low status of the skill entitled 'Working with Others' is demonstrated by the lack of reference to this type of learning in the programmes of study.

It is clear that the purpose of assessment of social literacy must be to focus on the individual child, and that assessment at this individual level is the primary concern. The development of social literacy is itself a product of reflection on the self, and on analysis of social interaction. It is not the result of a particular taught curriculum. The development of the individual relies on scaffolded (Vygotsky 1978) learning, and that in turn requires formative feedback. Children cannot realize the consequences of their actions unless those are reported back for them to reflect on. Thus assessment of social development must be a continual, formative process. This allows children to develop as moral individuals, through feedback from the social context within which they are growing up. It must be an inclusive type of assessment, which allows all children to claim success in a wide range of fields. Social competence, and the social virtues (Chapter 2) can be displayed by adults and children in vastly differing social situations, and for the child's development in this area to be meaningful and co-ordinated, evidence needs to be drawn from all aspects of children's lives, both within and without the school. Many schools already recognize children's achievements outside school in informal ways, and home–school contact books and diaries are acknowledged as important ways of providing continuity between children's learning at home and at school. The proposed model could build on this.

It was suggested in Chapter 4 that the four foci of Bottery (1990) – self-esteem, empathy, co-operation and rationality – should be adopted as a framework for social literacy. These four foci will lead to children displaying behavioural, cognitive, affective and meta-cognitive evidence of their learning. This further mitigates against the narrowing-down of assessment into testing, or other summative techniques. But it also provides rich opportunities for children and adults to be involved in a variety of types of assessment, which 'allow for diverse modes of response or multiple ways to demonstrate understanding' (Krechevsky and Seidel 1998: 30). Gardner (1993) is critical of the overemphasis in much assessment on linguistic and logical-mathematical intelligences, and proposes models which examine children's confidence and competence in other domains. There is no need for the sole assessor of children's social development to be the overworked class teacher. Additional adults with responsibility for the child's learning, such as learning support assistants, midday supervisors, sports coaches and parents, can make vital contributions to the evidence base.

But the most significant emphasis in assessing social literacy must lie with the children themselves. If two of the foci of attention in this area of learning are self-esteem and rationality, then meta-cognitive reflection and assessment must have centrality. Novak and Gowin (1983) and Watson (1996) in particular stress the benefits to learners of such emphases, and Stow (1997) has indicated how techniques such as concept mapping can have a beneficial effect on self-esteem. But children can also be involved in assessing each other, partly as a way of learning more about their own development. Chen *et al.* (1998) have shown how children as young as 4 years old can have sophisticated understandings of the social maps of their learning environments. Such mapping, and other peer-assessment techniques, provide the adults working alongside them with evidence too. But the formative aspect of the model is equally important. The Assessment Reform Group (1999) states that research indicates improvements in learning through assessment can be due to

> five simple factors: the provision of effective feedback to pupils; the active involvement of pupils in their own learning; adjusting teaching to take account of the results of assessment; a recognition of the profound influence assessment has on the motivation and self-esteem of pupils, both of which are crucial influences on learning; and the need for pupils to be able to assess themselves and understand how to improve.
>
> (1999: 4–5)

The National Advisory Committee on Creative and Cultural Education (DfEE 1999a) has called for the government to place a 'greater emphasis on formative assessment' (218, ii). Littledyke and Huxford (1998) stress the value to constructive learning of formative assessment, as a way of informing planning and providing feedback information to pupils. The model proposed for assessing social literacy is formative, continual and ipsative-referenced.

The idea of a 'six point scale' of moral development has been criticized by Bottery (1990), and it is proposed here that such a fixed scale for social literacy would be equally inappropriate. One of the crucial aspects of learning in this area is surely that it should be non-competitive and that it should not be norm-referenced. There is no possibility of a definition of the 'average' good person, nor any value in comparing one child's behaviour openly with another. Such comparisons are nearly always harmful to the child who is seen in a less favourable light ('Why can't you be polite, like your sister?'). The most appropriate model for referencing is ipsative. Children should be measuring their social development in comparison with themselves, albeit that they will draw on social criteria or 'norms' to make those measurements. Inman *et al.* (1998) contend that assessing personal and social development is undertaken to establish individual starting points for learning, and that comparisons between children are not possible because contexts are so different. The purpose of education in social literacy is to improve the child's understanding of, and ability to interact with, the particular society around them. Targets can be expressed in similar terms to different children, and categories of learning can have continua of development. But attaching numerical scales to these is counter-productive. In any case, Parziale and Fischer (1998) argue that children develop and regress in all areas of skill development. This is certainly the case in social development, where adults and children move backwards and forwards continuously along lines, or through areas of social competence. In view of earlier comments about linear progression in learning, perhaps talk of lines and continua is unhelpful. 'Fields of development' might be a more constructive phrase. The use of ipsative referencing also allows for the assessment model to be inclusive. There is little value in using strictly fixed criterion-referencing along normative scales with children who have difficulties in social and emotional learning. Ipsative referencing can place greater reward on self-improvement against previous 'performance', and can allow different children to achieve at their own levels. There will, of course, be a need for criteria against which children are assessed, and in most schools fixed frameworks, such as school rules, provide absolute boundaries to children's behaviour. These will form part of the criteria for assessment.

In common with most models of formative assessment, this model needs to be a continual process. Some of the evidence gathered could be used for summative purposes, such as report-writing, parental interviews or liaison, or whole-school monitoring, but the process of assessment and feedback should be one which follows the children throughout their school careers, and into adult life. As with National Records of Achievement, portfolios of evidence in social development should be of interest to potential employers and higher education recruitment. Research also suggests (Walters *et al.* 1994; Novak and Gowin 1983; Stow 1997) that periodic reviews of assessment evidence can highlight progression very clearly to the pupils themselves. Evidence can be gathered from a wide variety of contexts, including the child's experiences outside school. Within school, the contexts should be domain-specific (within curriculum subjects, and learning that is particular to those subjects) and generic (in any area of learning). It has already been indicated that the four foci of learning in social development (Bottery 1990) can provide behavioural, cognitive and affective evidence of children's development. Thus the assessment model should allow opportunities for children to display skills, understanding and attitudes in social literacy, as well as appropriate behaviour which demonstrates this learning. A variety of methods can be used to obtain evidence, including observation, performance tasks such as discussion and presentations, portfolios, and self-assessment and review (Krechevksy and Seidel 1998). Table 6.1 summarizes the model.

The Model in Detail

Before looking at each aspect of the model in detail, it is important to recognize that certain conditions need to be in place in schools, and certain shared understandings of ethos, before such a model could be used. It could be

Table 6.1 Defining Characteristics

Categories	Definition
Type of assessment	Formative (social constructivist)
Referencing	Ipsative (criterion)
Assessors	Children (self and peer), other adults, teachers
Contexts	Various – domain specific/generic; extra-curricular; outside school
Focus	Behavioural, cognitive (and meta-cognitive), affective; skills, understanding, attitudes
Methods	Various – observation, tasks, portfolios, self-assessment and review
Framework	Bottery's (1990) four foci – self-esteem; co-operation and empathy; rationality
Time	Continual throughout schooling

argued that ipsative forms of assessment have limited validity, since they do not allow for clear comparisons to be made between pupils. Furthermore, some schools and teachers might well be unhappy with the idea of negotiating criteria for assessment with pupils, particularly in such a sensitive area as social development. But it has been argued that a democratic school ethos, in which pupils genuinely participate in the running of an institution, is essential to provide the kind of context within which pupils can openly and fully reflect on social interactions. Participation and action, as suggested by Skillen (1997), is an essential aspect of developing social literacy. Griffith (1998) has also raised sharp questions about the possibility of developing pupils' critical autonomy and rationality without allowing for their participation and choice in decision-making at various levels. Studies of effective schools in disadvantaged communities (NCE 1996) stress the importance of providing 'inclusive' contexts: 'It has ... been recognised that these are crucial ways of enhancing the self-esteem of pupils and raising their levels of competence as learners' (1996: 328). Osler (1999) and Richardson (1998) stress the importance of providing inclusive practice in all areas of schooling as a powerful way of combating prejudice and racism. Thus, it could be contended that schools which are not prepared to embrace an inclusive, ipsative model of assessment for social literacy are not going to be genuinely committed to this area of children's learning. They may be more interested in it as a vehicle for didactic moral instruction.

The following section provides a clearer outline of the content of the model. Each section is based on one or more of Bottery's (1990) foci, and under each heading there is a preliminary discussion of issues for debate, an outline of what is being assessed, and a discussion of how and by whom it is being assessed.

Self-esteem

Assessment of this aspect of children's social development is mainly concerned with affective response, measured meta-cognitively. It could be said to measure Gardner's (1984) 'intrapersonal intelligence', although inevitably children will measure their self-esteem in part through analysis of their experiences in society. Thus it will touch also on areas of 'interpersonal intelligence'.

Issues

There are real problems in attempting to measure self-esteem. In the first instance, Dewhurst (1991) has contested whether or not teachers should be involved in promoting pupils' self-esteem at all, as this leads some children to make unfavourable comparisons of themselves with their peers. He argues for self-acceptance as a preferable alternative. Nesbitt (1993) argues that it is not in measuring self-esteem that we are in error, but in what it is about self-esteem that we choose to measure. He argues that children should be involved in measuring and thus defining their self-esteem through moral characteristics. Statman (1993) proposes that self-esteem will inevitably be measured by pupils in relation to tangible achievements which they compare with those of their peers. He suggests that, rather than ignoring this, teachers should explore the thinking that lies behind the pupil who has low self-esteem, and tackle it head-on. McNamara (1998: 18) reports Beck in a study published in 1976 as having identified a number of common systematic errors in logical thinking which can lead to people having a low self-esteem:

1 *Arbitrary inference*: a tendency to arbitrarily conclude from one event to another event which is not justified by the facts of the situation
2 *Overgeneralisation*: a tendency to conclude from one event to other events without adequate information
3 *Selective abstraction*: a tendency to consider a complex event on the basis of one aspect of it
4 *Magnification and minimisation*: a tendency to exaggerate negative events and minimise positive ones
5 *Personalisation*: a tendency to assume responsibility for an event (usually negative) when there is no basis for doing so
6 *Dichotomous thinking*: a tendency to evaluate events in extreme categories.

Watson (1996) sees measuring and raising self-esteem as a crucial way of raising the levels of performance of pupils with learning difficulties, suggesting that the 'learned helplessness' that they display is often exacerbated by pupils expecting failure and adopting defeatist attitudes to work and problem-solving. McNamara (1998) advocates the pupil being clearly involved in the collection of data about self-esteem, as he points out that it is vital that the pupils themselves can see the improvements in their qualitative and quantitative responses to self-assessment. Hymel and Franke (1985) point to research undertaken by Kagan *et al.* (published in 1982) which indicates that although younger (7-year-old) children are often inaccurate in the way that they tend to overestimate their positive characteristics, their identification of undesirable characteristics can often be clearly correlated to the evaluations of peers and teachers. Pupils' self-reports are therefore considered to be of value in providing information on the acquisition of social literacy.

What is Being Assessed?

Pupils' self-confidence is a vital factor in their success in school. This will be influential in the way they tackle academic tasks, their attitudes towards learning, and in the way they form relationships with adults and children. There will of course be a number of factors affecting self-confidence – past experience in school, daily experiences at home and the extent to which they fit into peer groups outside the home. Thus it may be important to allow and even encourage pupils to differentiate between different aspects of self-confidence. Children from the age of 4 years old have been shown (Chen *et al.* 1998) to exhibit very different levels of self-confidence in a variety of different contexts. Thus it will be important to assess this in domain-specific and generic contexts. Ways in which pupils can describe their own self-image and self-confidence will be outlined in the next section, but there may be clues evident in observable behaviour which can be best assessed by adults. These clues could include the extent to which pupils are able to persist with challenges (Sylva 1994), their behaviour when faced with conflict and aggression, their ability to initiate activity with their peers and the types of relationships they form with adults.

How/By Whom?

There are a variety of simple ways of involving children in assessment of their self-esteem. With very young children, use of structured interviews may help them to verbalize or identify their preferences. Children under 7 years old should not be expected to analyze their feelings or responses to any great extent. The identification of preferences and of simple causes of likes and dislikes is the starting point for later analysis and discussion. Krechevksy (1998) proposes interviewing children while they use a model of the classroom, in which they can manipulate blocks pasted with pictures of the children and adults in the group around a mock-up of the learning environment. This is obviously to allow less confident children to express preferences and understanding. Questions to be asked of children in this setting include (Krechevsky1998: 135):

> Is that your favourite activity (as child moves self to a particular area of the class where she/he spends time playing or working)?

> Which one do you think you were best at? Why? Which one was hardest for you (in response to looking at pictures of class activities over previous days)?

Chen *et al.* (1998) give examples of observation records that can be used by adults to assess children's development. Using the High/Scope assessment categories (1998: 37), they focus on 'Initiative' and 'Social Relations' as markers of social development, and these can be used in part as indicators of self-esteem. They favour a developmental scale, which some may disagree with. In the context of 'Relating to other children', the scale is as follows (Chen *et al.*1998: 39):

> Child does not yet play with other children.
> Child responds when other children initiate interactions.
> Child initiates interactions.
> Child sustains interactions with other children.
> Child works on complex projects with other children.

It has been argued earlier that 'progression' in these areas may not follow a linear pattern, and that it is difficult to objectify such behaviour into a scale of development in any case.

Children from as young as 4 years old can complete their own preference sheets without the need to be able to interpret text. Digital photos of activities can be pasted onto sheets, with a series of faces depicting different responses to the activities – enjoyment, neutrality and anxiety are some possible types. These can then form the basis of subsequent interviews, which can be conducted by older children, other adults or teachers. Samples of these could be included in packs of parental link materials, such as the Project Spectrum Parent Activities Manual (Ramos-Ford 1998). Parents can thus be integrated into the assessment process, and will have important contributions to make to parental interviews.

As the children progress through school, the complexity of such exercises can increase, and children can increasingly complete assessment of their own self-esteem. In order to integrate the assessment activity fully with the learning process, children could be invited as a group to think of the factors which influence their self-image, and teachers can use these to inform evaluation and self-assessment sheets or tasks. McNamara (1998) has used Records of Self-Confidence with a pupil experiencing difficulties in school. These ask the pupil to record each week a percentage figure for their self-confidence in lessons. At the top of the sheet (McNamara 1998: 13) an indication of scale is given – 100% = at ease, enjoyed lesson; 50% neither particularly happy nor particularly upset; 0% = upset, felt sick, worried. Through using such a scale he was able (with expert advice) to 'facilitate a positive restructuring', addressing the false inferences the pupil was making about the lessons, and helping him to mark his self-confidence in a less generalized way. The results of the chart were plotted on a graph, and the visual representation of his improving confidence was said to have been an important factor in sustaining improvements and raising the pupil's awareness of this. Obviously, such a detailed and time-consuming practice might be deemed unnecessary, but it could be one of a number of strategies available to pupils and teachers in assessing self-esteem. Instead of focusing exclusively on academic lessons, children could discuss and negotiate the categories to be graded. Some teachers might rightly object that such a stark series of indicators might actually draw pupils' attention to areas in which they had not considered that they lacked confidence. There is a tendency for younger pupils in the 7–11 age range to have misplaced (but perhaps helpful) self-confidence in certain areas of learning, in part because the way these areas are assessed has not allowed them to make invidious comparisons with other subjects, in part because of the nature of learning in those areas, and in part because of their stage of development (Hymel and Franke 1985). The narrower the forms of learning and assessment in a given area, the more likely pupils are subsequently to generalize about their dislike of a subject. For example, pupils (and adults) may say 'I don't like Art, because I can't draw'. Such a statement is more often a product of the type of art education they have experienced than a true reflection of their aptitude for artistic learning. There is evidence that girls in particular tend to underestimate their abilities in academic learning and other areas (Oscarsson 1995), and teachers would need to be aware of this.

It will be important that pupils are not overburdened (as are some adult learners in higher education) with evaluation exercises, particularly those that ask them to examine their own feelings and personal responses to learning situations. Excessive use of these strategies will lead to loss of interest. A variety of strategies is required, to maintain interest and progression. The use of strategies needs to be spaced apart, and needs some kind of overall co-ordination and planned regularity. But, as indicated earlier (Krechevsky and Seidel 1998), the repetition of exercises is important for pupils to be able to recognize progress, and come to terms with regression (Parziale and Fischer 1998). Self-confidence and esteem is a fluctuating aspect of adult life, and will be so for children also. Repetition is also important to increase pupils' familiarity with the chosen strategies, and make them more comfortable with the whole process of self-assessment. Progression also needs to be built in to the pupil's experience, so that strategies used give the opportunity for increasingly detailed responses. That is not to say that techniques used with 4-year-olds may not be applied to older children, provided that the contexts of interaction are different (interviews) or that the expectation of greater sophistication in response is indicated (digital-photo like/dislike sheets). In particular, if the engine of assessment is negotiated with pupils, this negotiation and the final products may provide useful evidence for teacher and pupil assessment of their ability to think meta-cognitively.

In secondary schools (NCE 1996), systems of personal tutoring, and the keeping of diaries and personal logs, have proved to be effective ways of promoting self-esteem. In most primary schools, the main provider of pastoral support is also the class teacher, so such a system is less likely to be necessary.

Co-operation and Empathy

Under this heading, children and adults will be reflecting more on behavioural aspects of children's social literacy, although the affective and cognitive dimension will also be significant. This is where the social interaction of the pupils will be the evidence base for assessment, and thus it is the 'interpersonal intelligence' (Gardner 1984) that is being measured. It is in this area that children will most effectively be able to display behaviour that demonstrates their social competence, and their adoption of 'social virtues' (Chapter 2).

Issues

A number of issues will determine whether or not this area can be effectively assessed. For children to display co-operative behaviour, the school will have to provide a curriculum context which values co-operative and collaborative working. It has already been indicated (Chapter 4) that the wording of the National Curriculum (QCA 1999b) does not appear to encourage this, and that research (Galton *et al.* 1999) into teaching and learning styles in primary classrooms has shown a scarcity of such contexts. It is incumbent on schools which are committed to developing social literacy to look for opportunities for collaborative learning on a regular basis, and in a variety of subjects, so that pupils can develop their skills in this area (Watson 1996). They should then also develop their ability to reflect on their co-operative skills, and come to see this as an essential part of their learning. Much good practice exists already in schools in PSHE, such as the widely used technique of 'Circle Time'. But opportunities for social learning and reflection are available in all curriculum subjects, and all teachers can testify to the rich-ness of learning that can take place in such settings. 'Group work' such as that outlined in some aspects of the National Literacy Strategy (DfEE 1998b) is not *necessarily* a genuinely collaborative exercise. Teachers need to be certain that problems can only be solved by a group, and that children need to work effectively as a team, before group activities can be described as collaborative. There are of course many other aspects of school life which provide examples of co-operative or empathetic behaviour and attitudes. Playtime break/recess is a gold mine of information about children's ability to get on with each other, and their propensity to help each other out (Faulkner 1997). Official structures, such as school councils, prefect systems or class monitor rotas, can also show children taking on responsibilities and helping others. In Japan and other education systems in the Far East, 'service' is an explicit aspect of schooling. Children learn to take turns cleaning the school, serving dinners to peers and undertaking other community responsibilities. In England, many schools provide similar informal opportunities, and work in the community outside the school is also encouraged. However, recognition for work that is not organized through the school is less frequently given, although many children, through organizations such as Scouts and Girl Guides, sports clubs and informally within their own neighbourhoods, are involved on a regular basis in altruistic work. It will, therefore, be essential for schools to negotiate the precise contexts for assessing this area of social development with pupils, staff and the local community, so that a wide evidence base can be drawn on.

What is Being Assessed?

Co-operation and co-operative skills are regularly assessed by teachers on an informal basis. They observe children sharing resources, taking turns to answer questions, helping peers with work and playing together. There are any number of actions that children can perform which give indications of their ability to collaborate and co-operate. This ability can be seen in children (despite Piaget?) of as young as 3 years old. Children receive powerful messages from the adults around them that co-operation is one of the key social skills, and they are keen to demonstrate this behaviour. Toddlers gain approval for handing round a tube of Smarties before they tuck in themselves, and even infants gain pleasure from offering food back to the carer who is feeding them. Empathy, however, is a much less visible 'quality', as it is more of an attitude or affective response than a behavioural attribute. It may be supposed as the basis for certain altruistic actions, but is more likely to be evident in discussions about social situations and dilemmas, or later in children's imaginative writing and role-play. With older primary children and with secondary-age pupils, exploring the word and possible definitions may well lead to interesting and varied views on how it can be assessed. Children's empathetic behaviour and attitudes may well be evident only over a considerable period of time. Summative assessments of this aspect of their social development will be very difficult to undertake.

How/By Whom?

A number of different methods can be employed to assess these areas, and a wide range of people can bring important evidence to bear. In domain-specific settings, teachers can set questions and activities for discussion which demand empathetic thinking from the children. Don Rowe's pack, *You, Me, Us* (Citizenship Foundation 1994) is an excellent example of a purpose-built curriculum programme, which generates discussion of social and personal issues, and at the same time allows children to demonstrate developing ability in engaging in social and co-operative behaviour. Rowe talks of the stories in the pack having 'focuses of concern' including 'self, self and others, other people, other people (the group) and the group, community or society'. He argues that the discussion and follow-up to the stories allows children to demonstrate their ability to think at these various levels. Drama work in History (Wilson and Woodhouse 1990) can also provide opportunities for children to display empathetic thinking. Children can also be given the chance to display co-operative skills in collaborative practical work, or in paired or group problem-solving in any subject. Teachers will observe and document their development in these areas through their standard methods of assessment.

However, the involvement of children in peer and self-assessment of this area can be the richest source of evidence. Children should first be asked, in age-appropriate language, to discuss the dimensions of co-operation. This may lead to a group list of examples of co-operative behaviour (or 'being kind to/helping other people' for younger children). Using these criteria, a number of methods can be employed. Asher (1985) reports the use of socio-metric measures with children, where they are asked to rate their peers along an attitudinal scale of 1–5, as a way of identifying the skills training needs of 'unpopular children' (1985: 158). Such measures might appear rather brutal in a primary classroom, but it will depend on the questions being asked, and the descriptors of the scale. If children are asked to respond positively to questions, they may be able to draw positive social maps of the class or group. An imaginative example of such an exercise being employed with pre-school children is the Project Spectrum Classroom Model (Krechevsky 1998). The model of the classroom is built, 2 ft by 3 ft, and filled with accurate representations of the furnishings of the room, and blocks pasted with pictures (2 inches tall for children and 3 inches tall for adults) to represent the people. Children are then asked various questions, initially about their preferred activities, but later about their perceptions of their peers. For example, children can be asked 'Who would you go to for help if you hurt yourself?', or 'If the teacher was sick for a day, which child would you choose to take over?' Asking them to map friendship groups in the class can also demonstrate their understanding of the social map of the group. With older children, such models of the classroom, dinner hall or playground could provide opportunities to discuss disputes or difficulties that may be occurring in those situations, and allow children to show their ability to mediate in conflicts or find solutions to social problems. A further method advocated by Project Spectrum is a 'Peer Interaction Checklist' (1998: 144). This is a list of twenty-nine behaviours, which it is suggested will incorporate the seven to nine that most children will display to represent their 'role definition' (there are four roles: Team Player, Facilitator, Leader and Independent Player). The behaviours include:

* mediates when conflicts occur;
* spends a lot of time observing the play of other children;
* often extends and elaborates other people's ideas;
* expresses concern about whether or not she is being accepted by other children.

A summary sheet is provided which categorizes children's behaviour under the headings of the role definitions. The precise categories used in this instance may not be to the liking of all teachers, but the idea could be adapted to the classroom context, and a simplified version of the list could even be used or devised by older children for them to undertake observation in their own or others' classrooms. Building this into the PSHE programme of a Year 6 or 6th grade class could be very beneficial to children's learning in this area, particularly if these older children undertake observation of infant or kindergarten classes (with children they are mentoring) and subsequently reflect on children's development in this area.

Returning to the negotiated criteria of co-operative behaviour, children can represent these as areas of development or lines of progression, and analyze their own behaviour within a particular field. In discussion with a partner (an ideal and increasingly rare opportunity for mixed-ability pairings?) they can identify occasions when they have displayed the behaviour that they consider to be co-operative, and highlight opportunities for this in the future. They can then set targets for themselves, in their own contexts, which can be reviewed as part of PSHE work, or informally, on a regular basis. If this is recorded, either through a scribe (another adult or an able writer) or independently, children can then keep diaries or portfolios, which they use to claim evidence of appropriate behaviour. The process of choosing methods of recording could help develop children's learning in ICT and Design Technology. Signatories could be parents and carers, other adults in the community such as church leaders or sports coaches, additional adults in the school, teachers and their peers. These signatories could also propose 'credits' to the teacher on behalf of a pupil, particularly younger children or those lacking in self-confidence or awareness. This system can work effectively through mentoring, where older children are paired with younger, and help them to review targets alongside a class teacher or learning support assistant. Evidence of particular personal attainment in this area can be celebrated at a class or school level, thus raising the status of such social behaviour as a highly regarded aspect of community life. But it is vital that the criteria for success in this model are defined by the child, as what may be regarded as significant for one child may be less so for another. The purpose of the assessment would be to provide positive evidence and feedback to the child of attainment in this area. It is suggested that negative aspects of behaviour should be recorded elsewhere.

Such a model could be extended into secondary education as it stands, or receive a more formal status through recorded testimonies, from peers and adults, in National Records of Achievement. Such portfolios ought to be able to provide rich evidence to prospective employers or schools of a child's development in social literacy.

Rationality

This final area of assessment contains two fields: it will focus on children's knowledge and understanding of society and communities (at group, class, school, local and national levels); and it will examine their meta-cognition, or their ability to undertake reflection on their own learning, academic and social, and on their self-esteem.

Issues

For there to be abundant evidence of children's abilities in these areas, a substantial commitment is required to promoting higher-order thinking in all subjects. This may mean at primary level that teachers need to go beyond the remit of the National Curriculum. It was indicated in Chapter 4, how critical questioning of subjects appears to be restricted in subjects like Science, DT and ICT to mid-adolescence. Yet young children are perfectly capable of making critical comment and raising important ethical and moral questions, particularly in fields that are relevant to their concerns. There is ample evidence, for example, of children's ability to interact critically with all media, and with consumer products and promotions. They are also often able to articulate real concerns about social and moral dimensions of learning in Geography (especially in relation to the environment), History and RE. Higher-order thinking can also be demonstrated in children's analysis of their own learning strategies, and in them being given a certain amount of control over their learning. In the current climate, few would advocate the levels of independence and choice that Griffith (1998) would like to see them exerting over their own curriculum. But less extreme versions of this giving of autonomy to pupils have been reported (NCE 1996) as being a factor in raising self-esteem and raising standards in disadvantaged areas.

Social Knowledge and Critical Thinking

What is Being Assessed?

Children develop understanding of society and social values through their learning in a number of subjects – aspects of this have been more clearly outlined in Chapter 4. They will be most likely to display cognitive evidence of this through their written and oral responses to specific tasks. Progression in this understanding will be evident in a number of ways – in the increasing complexity of questions raised and analysis provided; in the increasing detail of answers to, in particular, historical and geographical questions about society itself; and in increasingly sophisticated responses to specific discussions in PSHE and Citizenship, such as those initiated by the Citizenship Foundation pack (1994). Contributions to debates and Circle Time discussion will also provide evidence of a range of different levels of understanding. This is the one aspect of children's understanding of social literacy which *could* be graded, and which can be assessed quite effectively through summative methods.

A further and equally important aspect of children's rationality, which may affect their ability to fit in with the social environment, is 'Practical Intelligence' (Gardner *et al.* 1998). In Gardner's applied version, this covers three areas: managing themselves; managing tasks; and co-operating with others. It was shown in Chapter 4 how children at pre-school gain significant social benefit from being introduced to such practical intelligence training at a very young age. The success of the High/Scope 'graduates' in this area has been well documented (Ball 1994). The PIFS programme (Gardner and Krechevksy 1993) indicates the potential of similar programmes, when properly implemented by highly trained teachers, to raise pupil effectiveness. Improvement was most marked here in subject-specific aspects, such as managing subject tasks.

How/By Whom?

For the first time in this model, it seems less appropriate for children to be involved in the assessment of their learning. Much of the evidence of developing rationality will be assessable through formative and summative teacher assessment. Children's understanding of the social and affective aspects of subject learning will be assessed through the usual methods – marking written work, observing discussions and assessing projects and oral presentations. Drama work, and children's explanations of the rationale behind their creative work, can also provide evidence of critical thinking. Work in Design Technology and ICT can allow them to demonstrate awareness of social needs in context. It will be important that criteria for such assessments are made clear to the children, so that they see this as an important aspect of their work. Rowe (Citizenship Foundation 1994: 19) gives various indicators of rationality that can be observed in children's PSHE/Citizenship discussions: 'clarity of thought and expression; higher order reasoning skills; more generalized or abstract thinking; ability to analyze, utilize, apply or reformulate ideas; and more complex moral reasoning'. To this could be added: the ability of the child to adopt a position other than his/her own in role-play or debate. Plenary sessions in all subjects offer rich contexts for the assessment of critical thinking, provided that there is a classroom ethos of encouraging children to make constructive, critical comment on their own and peers' work.

The PIFS programme (Gardner and Krechevsky 1993) offers a model of interview which could be undertaken by teachers or learning support assistants. It helps teachers to identify which pupils have weaknesses in the areas of practical intelligence outlined above. Of more immediate use perhaps is a model of assessment tasks (Gardner *et al.* 1998) which assesses the key areas of practical intelligence, or study skills. Children can be given three types of task (definitional, task-oriented and meta-task) – examples are as follows (1998: 120):

UNDERSTANDING QUESTIONS

Student [*sic*] is asked to imagine that she is a teacher, and that one of her pupils has handed in a research-report [*sic* – for UK, read project] which is copied directly from the text-books. Student writes dialogue between herself and the pupil in which she convinces the pupil not to copy.

TASK-ORIENTED QUESTIONS

Student is given a stack of unorganised school papers and asked to put them in order, paper-clipping the ones that belong together, and giving each paper-clipped stack a category label.

REFLECTION QUESTIONS

Student is presented with another student's suggestions for altering the school curriculum; student is asked to write down the advantages/disadvantages to making such changes.

The authors do not claim any significant degree of originality in these proposals, but they seem to offer a simple series of tasks for assessing children's study skills. Such assessments are probably rarely undertaken in UK primary schools, but when there is a curriculum which is increasingly subject-divided in an employment culture which demands people with transferable learning skills, perhaps these activities and the learning programmes that go with them have a place.

There may even be a place here for knowledge-based assessments of children's understanding of the important features of society. Such assessments (Kerr 1999b) are undertaken at a national level in some countries – Sweden has tests for 12-year-olds – and as part of a national sampling process in others (Korea, Holland, Hungary and Spain). Schools will have to decide for themselves whether this aspect of the PSHE/Citizenship curriculum guidelines has a key place in developing social literacy.

Meta-cognition

The importance of recognizing this aspect of children's learning has been frequently stressed (Flavell 1985; Bonnett 1994; Watson 1996), and methods for assessing it are continually being devised. Attention has already been drawn to the work of Novak and Gowin (1983) in this area, but all the methods of assessment so far proposed in this chapter can provide evidence of children's thinking about their thinking.

What is Being Assessed?

There are two areas of assessment here. Both are focused on cognitive development, but can also be found in affective responses to certain activities. In generic terms, pupils are being assessed for their ability to undertake any kind of self-reflection activity, and in particular on general aspects of their personal, social and emotional development. To what extent can they distance themselves from their own work and talk, and analyze it critically? Work here could be extended to mean structured and unstructured play, social interaction, relationships with peers and adults, and co-operative and community-based actions. In domain-specific terms, the assessment is of the pupils' ability to reflect critically on their learning in particular subjects. A child may have an advanced level of proprioception in Physical Education, but find it difficult to self-correct and redraft work in English. Another may have a sophisticated awareness of criteria for aesthetic judgement in Art or Music, but be comparatively unable to criticize their own methods for calculating a mathematical problem. In this area, the programmes of study for the National Curriculum are more helpful: children are required to be critical of their own and others' work in many subjects, even at Key Stage 2. Teachers may therefore find the level descriptions in those subjects help them to describe the performance of pupils. In order to assess such thinking, techniques such as concept or mind-mapping and spider diagrams may assist teachers in providing a context for questioning children (Stow 1997). There is considerable emphasis in the National Numeracy Strategy (DfEE 1999b) on pupils being asked to explain their thinking in Mathematics. By building evaluation time into collaborative work in all subjects, teachers can allow children to demonstrate their ability to reflect on the effectiveness of their work. Younger children often find it easier to develop the language of self-reflection through learning to offer comments on other children's ideas first.

How/By Whom?

The teacher has an important role in the collection of evidence from all the sources suggested above – like/dislike charts, interviews, portfolios, self-confidence charts and surveys, observation forms – to make assessment of the pupil's general ability to undertake meta-cognitive reflection. Quality of work will be evident in the detail of comment or claims made, and the depth of analysis the pupil has been able to undertake. Inevitably some normative comparisons will be made across a group of children, but the function of this assessment should be mainly formative, to provide individual feedback to the pupil. The evidence may also inform summative report-writing at key points in a school year. A summary comment sheet, with formative targets, could perhaps be added to a portfolio, for the child to take on to the following year. More specific evidence can be scrutinized in subject learning. The teacher may collect examples of work such as concept maps, initial and subsequent brainstorms and comments, and any other evidence of reflection in a particular subject. This will enable specific feedback to be given to the pupil in that area, and help the teacher to build up a clearer picture of the areas of learning in which the pupil has reflective strengths.

The final strand of this assessment involves the pupils reflecting on their ability to think meta-cognitively. Interviews, following up the use of techniques such as concept mapping, can provide evidence to the teacher of the pupil's ability to engage in such reflection, and helps the pupil to see how to improve future attempts (Stow 1997). At review points in the year, form tutors or class teachers could organize the children to discuss the strategies they use for meta-cognitive reflection, and their various merits. Questions can be asked, such as 'How do you feel about being asked to [technique or strategy can be inserted here]'?, or 'Did you find it easy filling in these sheets? How useful are they?' Open-ended questions are obviously better for discussion, while questions demanding response along a numerical or attitudinal scale need to be closed. These 'reflection on reflection' activities are probably best undertaken with older primary or secondary pupils only if done at a review point. Younger children would need to be asked the questions as they used the particular techniques. The value of this obviously depends on the frequency of use of meta-cognitive tasks. If the children are comparatively unfamiliar with this type of learning, they will not possess the language or conceptual understanding to dissect it. But familiarity will breed confidence, and go some way towards helping the children acquire 'mastery' rather than 'helplessness' (Sylva 1994) over their learning. The importance of meta-level knowledge of discourses was stressed in Chapter 3 (pp. 30–4).

Conclusions

The above model is designed to provide a series of strategies for gaining diverse information about children's aptitudes and achievements in social literacy. It may seem to some an onerous collection, but by placing the emphasis on children and other adults being central to the process, it is believed that burdens on class teachers will be minimal. More importantly, this emphasis on children as the primary assessors has been shown to enhance their social learning. It is by observing the social behaviour of those around us that we learn to become social beings, and this process carries an expectation for children to make discriminating observations and comments on key areas of social competence. By involving children from the youngest age, we build up a base of skill in this area, and an expectation that this is one of the key purposes of schooling. Children are very aware of this in informal ways, through the praise and censure they receive from their teachers, parents and adult supervisors for their behaviour. But by giving their development in this area formal assessment status, we are surely going to send out important signals about the status of this area of learning. The relationship between curriculum importance and assessment status has been thoroughly discussed elsewhere, and the starkest evidence of this is that the general public may sometimes know little else about a school than its position in core subject league tables.

For this status to be achieved, and for social literacy to be an important and permanent aspect of learning in school, a number of factors need to be in place. As described above, there needs to be an established assessment framework in each class, alongside a commitment from teachers to maintaining pupil involvement in this area of assessment. But this commitment needs to be sustained across a whole team of teachers and, perhaps most importantly, shared by the head teacher and the governors. On a wider scale, there is a need too for something of a change in culture in the OFSTED inspection framework. Unsurprisingly, OFSTED concentrate on linear progression in learning as represented by the school's implementation of the National Curriculum. There is mention of inspecting ethos, and of the contribution that extra-curricular work makes to the children's development. Spiritual, moral, social and cultural development are also given some prominence. But, as in the curriculum itself, there is insufficient emphasis on the children's learning to work collaboratively and co-operatively, despite the overwhelming importance given to this skill in most aspects of adult social interaction at work and at play. As Learmonth (1997: 59) states: 'We have valued what we can measure easily; we must learn urgently to measure all the qualities we value.' The reporting of excellence in this area needs to be given far greater priority. It is striking that there is a plethora of initiatives to highlight schools' successes in developing basic skills. One such is called 'Quality Mark' where schools can apply to receive the 'Quality Mark' status for their skill in promoting children's abilities in literacy and numeracy. There are 'Beacon School' titles awarded to particular schools for similar reasons, schools that are rightly held up to other institutions as models of good teaching and learning. Why not 'Beacon Schools' for social literacy, or PSHE and Citizenship, which is arguably what parents and the community value most in a school? Ask neighbours of a school what they most admire in the pupils that walk past their house every day, and they will not talk glowingly of SATs results, or status in league tables. They will want to discuss the manners and politeness of the children. The social development of the child is often the primary concern of parents attending open evenings or parental interviews. How about a 'Quality Mark' for schools which do outstanding work in the community, or are highly praised by OFSTED for their pastoral work and school ethos? Or an award of 'Investors in Pupils' to schools? Pring (1984: viii) highlights a widely used quotation, from an anonymous American high school principal, which ends with the lines: 'Help your students to become human. Your efforts must never produce learned monsters, skilled psychopaths, educated Eichmanns. Reading, writing, arithmetic are important only if they serve to make our children more human.' Unless social development is given high assessment status in schools nationally, it will become ever marginalized in the drive to raise the levels of performance of individual pupils in basic skills. If government initiatives in PSHE and Citizenship are to be genuinely educative, then they must be based on developmentally appropriate practice in this area. Assessment structures can sometimes drive the curriculum in the wrong direction. Raising 'standards', in the area of social literacy more than anywhere else, must not be for the purposes of public accountability. It must be for the benefit of the individuals being educated.

Two further commitments are needed. Firstly, there needs to be a change in emphasis in the curriculum at 3–6 years old. A strong emphasis needs to be placed in England, as it is in most other developed countries, on providing a richer context for *genuine* social learning for these children. The proven success of studies such as High/Scope (Ball 1994) depends on this, and on adequate funding and facilities being provided for such education. Young children need to learn in a number of different domains, using high-quality resources and with a wealth of adult support, through play, group and individual learning. Their learning in, through and about groups needs to be central to curriculum planning. It can be contended that an overemphasis on the individual and linear acquisition of basic skills, as represented in the current arrangements in England for Baseline Assessment (QCA 1998b) and the framework for inspection of nursery schools (OFSTED 1995), is counter-productive in the long-run. Children's socialization should be the primary goal of education at this stage.

Secondly, any change in emphasis in schools towards a greater emphasis on social literacy must be preceded by changes in initial teacher education. As Learmonth (1997) suggests, current teacher education in England often provides little or no study in PSHE – in teaching styles, learning or assessment strategies – as providers are obliged to cover an ever burgeoning syllabus for subject specialism, and subject-specific pedagogy. When teachers are occasionally the most trusted adult in a child's life, and when this is such a central aspect of the role of teacher, *in loco parentis*, this is a dangerous oversight. Stephenson (1998: 155), in an article exploring teacher and student teacher attitudes to Values Education, has suggested: 'If we believe there is a maturational process in the socio-moral awareness of children, then when their teachers are unable or unwilling to engage in dialogue on abstract principles it is unlikely that development in the classroom will take place.' She quotes an individual in the survey as saying: 'Values education? I don't hold with that – it's a waste of my time.' Such attitudes need to be changed, and initial teacher education is the ideal location to raise the status of the social dimensions of learning and assessment. As, laudably, an emphasis on values has been added to the curriculum for schools, so it must be reinserted into the curriculum for teacher education.

Bibliography

Abraham, J. (1993) *Divide and School: Gender and Class Dynamics in Comprehensive Education*, London: Falmer Press.

Aguado-Odina, T. (1993) 'Provision for Pre-school Children in Spain', in David, T. (ed.) *Educational Provision for our Youngest Children – European Perspectives*, London: Paul Chapman Publishing.

Ahier, J. and Ross, A. (1995) *The Social Subjects within the Curriculum: Children's Social Learning in the National Curriculum*, London: Falmer Press.

Anderson, V. (1998) 'Community Service Learning and School Improvement', *Phi Delta Kappa*, 72: 761–764.

Apple, M. (1995) *Education and Power*, 2nd edition, London: Routledge.

APU (Assessment and Performance Unit) (1980) *Personal and Social Development Dimensions*, APU.

Arnold, M. (1869) *Culture and Anarchy*, 1963 edition, London: Penguin.

Arthur, J. (1998) 'Communitarianism: What are the Implications for Education', *Educational Studies*, 24(3): 353–368.

—— (1999) *Schools and the Community*, London: Routledge/Falmer.

—— (2000) *Schools and Community: The Communitarian Agenda in Education*, London: Falmer Press.

Arthur, J. and Davison, J. (2000) 'Social Literacy and Citizenship Education in the School Curriculum', *The Curriculum Journal*, 11(1): 9–23.

Arthur, J., Davison, J. and Moss, J. (1997) *Subject Mentoring in the Secondary School*, London: Routledge.

Arthur, J., Gaine, S. and Walters, H. (2000) *Earthen Vessels: The Thomistic Tradition in Education*, Leominster: Gracewing.

Asher, S. (1985) 'An Evolving Paradigm in Social Skill Training Research with Children', in Schneider, B., Rubin, K. and Ledingham, J. (eds) *Children's Peer Relations: Issues in Assessment and Intervention*, New York: Springer-Verlag.

Assessment Reform Group (1999) *Assessment for Learning: Beyond the Black Box*, Cambridge: School of Education, Cambridge University.

Ball, C. (ed.) (1994) *Start Right: The Importance of Early Learning*, London: RSA.

Ball, S. (1981) *Beachside Comprehensive: A Case Study of Secondary Schooling*, London: Cambridge University Press.

—— (1985) 'English for the English', in Goodson, I. (ed.) *Social Histories of the Secondary Curriculum*, London: Falmer Press.

Bangs, J. (1996) 'A Culture Under Threat', *Education Review*, 10(1): 71–73.

Barber, M. (1991) *Partners for Change: Enhancing the Teaching Profession*, London: Institute for Public Policy Research.
—— (1992) 'An Entitlement Curriculum: A Strategy for the nineties', Journal of Curriculum Studies, 24 (5).
Bastiani, J. (1996) *Home–School Contracts and Agreements – Opportunity or Threat?*, London: RSA.
Beck, J. (1998) *Morality and Citizenship in Education*, London: Cassell.
Bell, G. (1998) 'The Personal Effectiveness Programme Initiative', *Journal of the National Association for Pastoral Care*, 16(2): 20–27.
Bennett, W. (1993) *The Book of Virtues: A Treasury of Great Moral Stories*, New York: Simon & Schuster.
Bentley, T. (1998) *Learning Beyond the Classroom: Education for a Changing World*, London: DEMOS/Routledge.
Bernstein, R. (1986) 'The Question of Moral and Social Development', in Cirillo, L. and Wapner, S. (eds) *Value Presuppositions in the Theories of Human Development*, London: Lawrence Erlbaum & Associates.
Best, R. (1999) 'The Impact of a Decade of Educational Change on Pastoral Care and Personal and Social Education: A Survey of Teacher Perceptions', *Journal of the National Association for Pastoral Care*, 17(2): 3–14.
BoE (Board of Education) (1904) *Regulations for Secondary Schools*, London: HMSO.
—— (1906) *Report on Questions Affecting Higher Elementary Schools*, London: HMSO.
—— (1910) *Circular 753*, London: HMSO.
—— (1911) *Report of the Committee on Housecraft in Girls' Secondary Schools*, London: HMSO.
—— (1913) *Report of the Committee on Practical Work in Secondary Schools*, London: HMSO.
—— (1919) *Teaching and Organising Secondary Schools*, London: HMSO.
—— (1921) *The Teaching of English in England* (Newbolt Report), London: HMSO.
—— (1923) *Report of the Consultative Committee on Differentiation of the Curriculum for Boys and Girls, Respectively*, London: HMSO.
—— (1926) *The Education of the Adolescent* (Hadow Report), London: HMSO.
—— (1938) *Report on Secondary Education* (Spens Report), London: HMSO.
Bonnett, M. (1994) *Children's Thinking: Promoting Understanding in the Primary School*, London: Cassell.
Bottery, M. (1990) *The Morality of the School: The Theory and Practice of Values in Education*, London: Cassell.
Bourdieu, P. (1973) 'Cultural Reproduction and Social Reproduction', in Brown, R. *Knowledge Education and Cultural Change*, London: Tavistock.
Burstyn, J. N. (1980) *Victorian Education and the Ideal of Womanhood*, London: Croom Helm.
Carr, D. (1991) *Educating the Virtues: An Essay in the Philosophical and Psychology of Moral Development and Education*, London: Routledge.
Carr, D. and Steutel, J. (eds) (1999) *Virtue Ethics and Moral Education*, London: Routledge.

Chen, J. Q., Krechevsky, M. and Viens, J. (1998) *Building on Children's Strengths: The Experience of Project Spectrum*, New York: Teachers College Press, Columbia University.

Citizenship Foundation (1994) *You, Me, Us*, London: Home Office.

Colberg-Schrader, H. and Oberhuemer, P. (1993) 'Early Childhood Education and Care in Germany', in David, T. (ed.) *Educational Provision for our Youngest Children – European Perspectives*, London: Paul Chapman Publishing.

Combs, M. and Slaby, D. A. (1977) 'Social Skills Training with Children', in Lahey, B., Crick, B. and Porter, A. (eds) *Political Education and Political Literacy*, London: Longman.

Connolly, J. A. and Doyle, A. B. (1984) 'The Relation of Social Fantasy Play to Social Competence in Pre-Schoolers', *Developmental Psychology*, 20: 797–806.

Corsaro, W. (1986) 'Discourse Processes Within Peer Culture: From a Constructivist to an Interpretative Approach to Childhood Socialisation', in *Sociological Studies of Child Development*, 1: 81–101.

Cottingham, J. (ed.) (1996) *Western Philosophy: An Anthology*, Oxford: Blackwell.

Davison, J. (1984) 'Language, Gender and Equality of Education for Girls', unpublished M.A. thesis, University of London.

—— (1997) 'Battles for English 1: 1870–1980', in Davison, J. and Moss, J. *Learning to Teach English in the Secondary School*, London: Routledge.

—— (2000) 'Literacy and Social Class', in Davison, J. and Moss, J. *Issues in English Teaching*, London: Routledge.

Davison, J. and Dowson, J. (1997) *Learning to Teach English in the Secondary School*, London: Routledge.

Davison, J. and Moss, J. (2000) *Issues in English Teaching*, London: Routledge.

Deci, E. (1995) *Why We Do What We Do*, New York: Putnam.

Deem, R. (1978) *Women and Schooling*, London: Routledge and Kegan Paul.

Dewey, J. (1933) *How we Think*, London: D. C. Heath.

—— (1938) *Experience and Education*, New York: Macmillan.

Dewhurst, D. (1991) 'Should Teachers Enhance Their Pupils' Self-Esteem?', *Journal of Moral Education*, 20(1): 11.

DfEE (Department for Education and Employment) (1995) *The National Curriculum*, London: HMSO.

—— (1998a) *Education for Citizenship and the Teaching of Democracy in Schools: Final Report of the Advisory Group in Citizenship*, London: QCA.

—— (1998b) *National Literacy Strategy*, London: DfEE.

—— (1999a) *All Our Futures: Creativity, Culture and Education*, London: DfEE.

—— (1999b) *The National Numeracy Strategy*, London: DfEE.

—— (1999c) *Report of the National Advisory Group on PSHE Preparing Young People for Adult Life*, London: DfEE.

Dixon, A. (1999) 'Preconceptions and Practice in Primary Citizenship Education', *Forum*, 41(1): 2–10.

Dunn, J. (1988) *The Beginnings of Social Understanding*, Oxford: Blackwell.

—— (1997) in Faulkner, D. 'Play, Self and the Social World', in Barnes, P. (ed.) *Personal, Social and Emotional Development of Children*, Oxford: Blackwell.

Durkheim, E. (1961) *Moral Education*, New York: Macmillan.

Dyhouse, C. (1978) 'Towards a Feminine Curriculum for English Schoolgirls: The Demands of Ideology 1870–1963', *Women's Studies Quarterly*, 1.

Bibliography

Eagleton, T. (1985) *Literary Theory: An Introduction*, Oxford: Basil Blackwell.

Eisner, E. (1984) *Cognition and Curriculum*, London: Longman.

Elliott, J. and Pring, R. (1975) *Social Education and Social Understanding*, London: University of London Press.

Evans, D. (1987) *Personal and Social and Moral Education in a Changing World*, London: NFER/Nelson.

Faulkner, D. (1997) 'Play, Self and the Social World', in Barnes, P. (ed.) *Personal, Social and Emotional Development of Children*, Oxford: Blackwell.

Fein, G. (1984) 'The Self-Building Potential of Pretend Play or "I got a fish, all by myself"', in Yawkey, T. D. and Pelegrini, A. D. (eds) *Child's Play: Developmental and Applied*, Hillsdale, NJ: Lawrence Erlbaum Associates.

Flavell, J. (1985) *Cognitive Development*, Englewood Cliffs, NJ: Prentice Hall.

Freire, P. (1972) *Pedagogy of the Oppressed*, Harmondsworth: Penguin.

—— (1985) *The Politics of Education: Culture, Power and Liberation*, London: Macmillan.

Frost, D. (1993) 'Reflective Mentoring and the New Partnership', in McIntyre, D. (ed.) *Mentoring*, London: Kogan Page.

Galton, M. *et al.* (1999) *Inside the Primary Classroom: 20 Years On*, London: Routledge.

Gardner, H. (1993) *Frames of Mind: The Theory of Multiple Intelligences*, New York: Basic Books.

Gardner, H. and Krechevsky, M.. (1993) 'Approaching School Intelligently: Practical Intelligence at the Middle School Level', in Gardner, H. *Multiple Intelligences: The Theory in Practice*, New York: Basic Books.

Gardner, H., Krechevsky, M, Sternberg, R. and Okagaki, L. (1998) 'Intelligence in Context: Enhancing Students' Practical Intelligence for Schools', in McGilly, K. (ed.) *Classroom Lessons: Integrating Cognitive Theory and Classroom Practice*, Cambridge, MA.: MIT Press.

Gaskell, J. (1985) 'Course Enrolment in High School: The Perspective of Working Class Females', *Sociology of Education*, 58: 48–59.

Gee, J. P. (1987) *The Social Mind: Language, Ideology and Social Praxis*, New York: Bergin & Garvey.

—— (1990) *Social Linguistics and Literacies: Ideology in Discourse*, London: Falmer Press.

—— (1992) 'What is Literacy?', in Shannon, P. (ed.) *Becoming Political*, Portsmouth, NH: Heinemann.

Giddens, A. (1994) 'Living in a Post-Traditional Society', in Beck, U., Giddens, A. and Lash, S. *Reflexive Modernisation: Politics, Tradition and Aesthetics in the Modern Social Order*, Cambridge: Polity Press.

Goldstrom, J. M. (1972) *Elementary Education 1780–1900*, London: David & Charles.

Goleman, D. (1996) *Emotional Intelligence*, London: Bloomsbury.

Goodson, I. (ed.) (1985) *Social Histories of the Secondary Curriculum*, London: Falmer Press.

Gosden, P. (1969) *How They Were Taught*, London: Blackwell.

Gossman, L. (1981) 'Literature and Education', *New Literary History*, l.

Griffith, R. (1998) *Educational Citizenship and Independent Learning*, London: Jessica Kingsley Publishers.

Gross, R. and Gross, B. (1969) *Radical School Reform*, Harmondsworth: Penguin.

Halsey, A. H. (1961) *Education, Economy and Society*, London: Collier Macmillan.

Hargreaves, D. (1967) *Social Relations in the Secondary School*, London: Routledge and Kegan Paul.

—— (1982) *The Challenge for the Comprehensive School: Culture, Curriculum and Community*, London: Routledge and Kegan Paul.

Haste, H. (1996) 'Communitarianism and the Construction of Morality', *Journal of Moral Education*, 25(1): 47–55.

Haydon, G. (1997) *Teaching about Values: A New Approach*, London: Cassell.

Her Majesty's Inspectorate (1984) *The Curriculum from 5 to 16*, London: HMSO.

Holden, C. (1999) ' "Hot Dinners and Netballs": Approaches to Social, Moral and Citizenship Education in Two Contrasting Schools', paper presented to Conference on Citizenship Education, Institute of Education, London.

Hollin, C. R. and Trower, P. (1988) 'Development and Application of Social Skills Training: A Review and Critique, in Hersen, M. *et al.* (eds) *Progress in Behaviour Modification*, 22, Newbury Park, CA: Sage.

Hoye, L. (1998) 'Let's Look at it Another Way: A Constructivist View of Art Education', in Littledyke, M. and Huxford, L. (eds) *Teaching the Primary Curriculum for Constructive Learning*, London: David Fulton.

Husen, T. and Postlethwaite, T. N. (eds) (1995) *International Encyclopedia of Education*, Oxford: Pergamon Books.

Hymel, S. and Franke, S. (1985) 'Children's Peer Relations: Assessing Self-Perceptions', in Schneider, B., Rubin, K. and Ledingham, J. (eds) *Children's Peer Relations: Issues in Assessment and Intervention*, New York: Springer-Verlag.

Inman, S., Buck, M. and Burke, H. (1998) *Assessing Personal and Social Development: Measuring the Unmeasurable?*, London: Falmer Press.

IRCA (International Review of Curriculum and Assessment) (1998) *International Review of Curriculum and Assessment Frameworks Project*, http://www.inca.org.uk/.

Jackson, B. and Marsden, D. (1962) *Education and the Working Class*, London: Routledge and Kegan Paul.

Kalantzis, M. and Cope, B. (1983) *An Overview: The Teaching of Social Literacy*, Sydney: Common Ground.

Kamm, J. (1971) *Indicative Past*, London: Allen & Unwin.

Kant, I. (1960) *Education*, Ann Arbor: University of Michigan Press.

Kelly, A. V. (1995) *Education and Democracy: Principles and Practices*, London: Paul Chapman Publishing.

Kelly, A. V. and Edwards, G. (1998) *Experience and Education: Towards an Alternative Curriculum*, London: Paul Chapman Publishing.

Kerr, D. (1999a) *Re-examining Citizenship: The Case of England*, Slough: NFER.

—— (1999b) 'The Citizenship Education Study', *International Review of Curriculum and Assessment Frameworks Project*, http://www.inca.org.uk/.

Kinsley, C. (1991) *Whole Learning Through Service*, Springfield, MA: Community Service Learning Centre.

Klein, J. (1965) *Samples from English Cultures*, London: Routledge and Kegan Paul.

Klug, F. and Spencer, S. (1998) 'Special Report: Education for Citizenship', *Multicultural Teaching*, 16(3): 43–45.

Bibliography

Kohlberg, L. (1984) *The Psychology of Moral Development*, San Francisco: Harper & Row.

Krechevsky, M. (1998) *Project Spectrum: Preschool Assessment Handbook*, New York: Teachers College Press, Columbia University (details at http://pzweb.harvard.edu/Research/Spectrum.htm).

Krechevsky, M. and Seidel, S. (1998) 'Minds at Work: Applying Multiple Intelligences in the Classroom', in Sternberg, S. and Williams W. (eds) *Intelligence, Instruction and Assessment: Theory into Practice*, Mahwah, NJ: Lawrence Erlbaum Associates.

Lahey, B., Crick, B. and Porter, A. (eds) (1974) *Political Education and Political Literacy*, London: Longman.

Lankshear, C. (1997) *Changing Literacies*, Buckingham: Open University Press.

Lawton, D. (1973) *Social Change, Educational Theory and Curriculum Planning*, London: Hodder & Stoughton.

Learmonth, J. (1997) ' "Rounded People and Active Members of the Community": Widening the Focus of the Curriculum', *Education Review*, 11(2): 56–60.

Likona, T. (1991) *Educating for Character – How Our Schools Can Teach Respect and Responsibility*, New York: Bantam.

Littledyke, M. and Huxford, L. (1998) *Teaching the Primary Curriculum for Constructive Learning*, London: David Fulton.

Macbeth, A. (1994) 'Involving Parents', in Moon, B. and Mayes, A. (eds) *Teaching and Learning in the Secondary School*, London: Routledge.

Mannheim, K. (1950) *Freedom, Power and Democratic Planning*, London: Routledge and Kegan Paul.

McIntyre, A. (1990) 'The Privatization of the Good', *Review of Politics*, 42.

McIntyre, D. (ed.) (1993) *Mentoring*, London: Kogan Page.

McLaughlin, T. (1992) 'Citizenship, Diversity and Education: A Philosophical Perspective', *Journal of Moral Education*, 21(3): 235–250.

—— (1995) 'Liberalism, Education and the Common School', *Journal of Philosophy of Education*, 29(2): 239–255.

McNamara, E. (1998) 'The Role of Thinking and Feeling: Extending Assessment Beyond Behaviour', *Journal of National Association for Pastoral Care in Education*, 16(2): 10–20.

Meadows, S. (1993) *The Development and Acquisition of Cognition in Childhood*, London: Routledge.

Mercer, N. (1995) *The Guided Construction of Knowledge*, Clevedon: Multilingual Matters.

Mill, J. S. (1909) *The Subjection of Women*, London: Longman.

Ministry of Education (1959) *Education Fifteen to Eighteen* (Crowther Report), London: HMSO.

—— (1963) *Half Our Future* (Newsom Report), London: HMSO.

Morrison, A. and McIntyre, D. (1971) *Schools and Socialisation*, Harmondsworth: Penguin.

Mulgan, G. (1997) *Connexity: How to Live in a Connected World*, London: Chatto & Windus.

Murray. L. (1996) 'Research into Social Purposes of Schooling', *Pastoral Care in Education*, 16(3): 28–35.

Musgrave, P. W. (1968) *The School as an Organization*, London: Macmillan.

Nash, R. J. (1997) *Answering the 'Virtuecrats': A Moral Conversation on Character Education*, Columbia University: Teachers College Press.

NCC (National Curriculum Council) (1989) *The National Curriculum*, London: DES.

—— (1990a) *Curriculum Guidance 3: The Whole Curriculum*, York: NCC.

—— (1990b) *Curriculum Guidance 4: Education for Economic and Industrial Understanding*, York: NCC.

—— (1990c) *Curriculum Guidance 6: Careers Education and Guidance*, York: NCC.

—— (1990d) *Curriculum Guidance 7: Environmental Education*, York: NCC.

—— (1990e) *Curriculum Guidance 8: Citizenship Education*, York: NCC.

NCE (National Commission on Education) (1993) *Learning to Succeed*, London: Heinemann.

—— (1996) *Success Against the Odds: Effective Schools in Disadvantaged Areas*, London: Routledge.

Neill, A. S. (1968) *Summerhill*, Harmondsworth: Penguin.

Nesbitt, W. (1993) 'Self-Esteem and Moral Virtue', *Journal of Moral Education*, 22(1): 51–53.

Novak, J. D. and Gowin, D. B. (1983) *Learning How to Learn*, Cambridge: Cambridge University Press.

OFSTED (Office for Standards in Education) (1995) *Guidance on the Inspection of Nursery and Primary Schools*, London: HMSO.

Oscarsson, V. (1995) 'Pupils' Views of the Future', in Osler, A. *et al.* (eds) *Teaching For Citizenship in Europe*, Stoke-on-Trent: Trentham Books.

Osler, A. (1999) 'Citizenship, Democracy and Political Literacy', *Multicultural Teaching*, 18(1): 12–15.

Parziale, J. and Fischer, K. (1998) 'The Practical Use of Skill Theory in Classrooms', in Sternberg, S. and Williams, W. (eds) *Intelligence, Instruction and Assessment: Theory into Practice*, Mahwah, NJ: Lawrence Erlbaum Associates.

Patten, J. (1992) 'Speech to Conservative Party Annual Conference', 7 October 1992.

Piaget, J. (1932) *The Moral Judgement of Children*, London: Routledge and Kegan Paul.

Popenoe, D., Norton, A. and Maley, B. (1994) *Shaping the Social Virtues*, Sydney: The Centre for Independent Studies.

Pring, R. (1975) *Social Education and Social Understanding*, London: University of London Press.

—— (1984) *Personal and Social Education in the Curriculum*, London: Hodder & Stoughton.

QCA (Qualifications and Curriculum Authority) (1998a) *Education for Citizenship and the Teaching of Democracy in Schools: Final Report of the Advisory Group on Citizenship*, London: QCA.

—— (1998b) *Baseline Assessment Pack*, London: QCA/DfEE.

—— (1999a) *Early Learning Goals*, London: DfEE/QCA.

—— (1999b) *The National Curriculum*, London: DfEE/QCA.

—— (1999c) *National Curriculum Handbook For Primary Teachers in England*, London: QCA/DfEE.

—— (1999d) *National Curriculum Handbook For Secondary Teachers in England*, London: QCA/DfEE.

Ramos-Ford, V. (1998) in Krechevsky, M. *Project Spectrum: Preschool Assessment Handbook*, New York: Teachers College Press, Columbia University.

Rennie, J. E., Lunzer, A. and Williams, W. T. (1974) 'Social Education: An Experiment in Four Secondary Schools', Schools Council Working Paper 51, London: Evans/Methuen.

Richardson, R. (1998) 'Inclusive Societies, Inclusive Schools – The Terms of Debate and Action', *Multicultural Teaching*, 16(2): 23–29.

Robertson, C. (1997) ' "I don't want to be independent." Does Human Life have to be Viewed in Terms of Potential Autonomy? Issues in the Education of Children and Young People with Severe, Profound and Multiple Learning Difficulties', in Fawkus, M. (ed.) *Children with Learning Difficulties: A Collaborative Approach to their Education and Management*, London: Whurr Publishers.

Robinson, T. and Shallcross, T. (1998) 'Social Change and Education for Sustainable Living', *Curriculum Studies*, 6(1): 69–84.

Rosen, B. C. and D'Andrade, R. (1959) 'The Pyschosocial Origins of Achievement Motivation', *Sociometry*, 22: 185–218.

Rowe, D. (1997) 'Value Pluralism, Democracy and Education for Citizenship', in Leicester, M., Modgil, C. and Modgil, F. (eds) *Values, Culture and Education: Political and Citizenship Education*, London: Cassell.

—— (1999) 'Public Discourse and its Emergence in the Primary Classroom as an Element of Citizenship Education – Implications for Teaching and Learning', paper presented to the Conference on Citizenship Education, London: Institute of Education.

Sampson, G. (1921) *English for the English*, London: Chapman & Hall.

Sandin, R. T. (1992) *The Rehabilitation of Virtue*, New York: Praeger.

SCAA (School Curriculum and Assessment Authority) (1996) *National Forum on Values and Community*, London: SCAA.

Schools Council (1971) *Social Education*, London: Evans/Methuen.

Schweinhart, L. J. and Weikart, D. P. (1994) in Ball, C. (ed.) *Start Right: The Importance of Early Learning*, London: RSA.

Schweinhart, L. J., Weikart, D. P. and Larner, M. (1986) 'Consequences of Three Pre-School Curriculum Models Through Age Fifteen', *Early Childhood Research Quarterly*, 1: 15–45.

Scrimshaw, P. (1975) 'The Language of Social Education', in Elliott, J. and Pring, R. (eds) *Social Education and Social Understanding*, London: University of London Press.

—— (1989) 'Prosocial Education', in Thacker, J., Pring, R. and Evans, D. (eds) *Personal and Social and Moral Education in a Changing World*, London: NFER/Nelson.

Sharpe, S. (1976) *Just Like a Girl*, London: Penguin.

Skillen, T. (1997) 'Can Virtue be Taught – Especially These Days', *Journal of Philosophy of Education*, 31(3): 375–393.

Skolverket (1998) *Curriculum for Pre-School*, http://www.skolverket.se/n/na.html.

Smith, H. *et al* (1993) *Can Virtue be Taught?*, Notre Dame, IN: University of Notre Dame Press.

Statman, D. (1993) 'Self-Assessment, Self-Esteem and Self-Acceptance', *Journal of Moral Education*, 22(1): 55–61.

Stephenson, J. (1998) 'A Perspective from England', in Stephenson, J., Ling, L., Bowman, E. and Cooper, M. (eds) *Values in Education*, London: Routledge.

Sternberg, R. J. (1985) *Beyond IQ*, Cambridge: Cambridge University Press.

Stow, W. (1996) 'Start Right – Start Early?', in Hayes, D. (ed) *Debating Education: Issues for the New Millennium*, Canterbury: Christ Church College.

—— (1997) 'Concept Mapping: A Tool for Self-Assessment?', *Primary Science Review*, 49: 12–15.

—— (2000) 'History: Values in the Diversity of Human Experience', in Bailey, R. (ed.) *Teaching Values and Citizenship Across the Curriculum: Educating Children for the World*, London: Kogan Page.

Straughan, R. (1988) *Can We Teach Children to be Good? Basic Issues in Moral, Personal and Social Education*, Milton Keynes: Open University Press.

Sylva, K. (1994) 'The Impact of Early Learning on Children's Later Development', in Ball, C. (ed.) *Start Right: The Importance of Early Learning*, London: RSA.

Tate, N. (1994) 'Off the Fence on Common Culture', *Times Educational Supplement*, 29 July.

—— (1996) 'The Role of the School in Promoting Moral, Spiritual and Cultural Values', *Education Review*, 10(1): 66–70.

Tobin, B. M. (1986) 'Development in Virtues', *Journal of Philosophy of Education*, 20(2): 201–214.

Turiel, E. (1983) *The Development of Social Knowledge: Morality and Convention*, New York: Cambridge University Press.

Turner, R. (1974) *Equality for Some*, London: Ward Lock.

Vygotsky, L. (1978) *Mind in Society: The Development of Higher Psychological Processes*, Cambridge, MA: Harvard University Press.

Walters, J., Seidel, S. and Gardner, H. (1994) 'Children as Reflective Practitioners: Bringing Metacognition into the Classroom', in Mangieri, J. and Collins Block, C. (eds) *Creating Powerful Thinking in Teachers and Students: Diverse Perspectives*, Orlando: Holt, Reinhart & Winston.

Watson, J. (1996) *Reflection Through Interaction: The Classroom Experience of Pupils with Learning Difficulties*, London: Falmer Press.

White, J. (1989) 'The Aims of Personal and Social Education', in White, P. (ed.) *Personal and Social Education: Philosophical Perspectives*, London: Kogan Page/The Bedford Way Series.

White, P. (1996) *Civic Virtues and Public Schooling*, New York: Teachers College Press.

Wilcox, B. (1997) 'Schooling, School Improvement and the Relevance of Alasdair McIntyre', *Cambridge Journal of Education*, 27(2): 249–260.

Wilcox, P. R. (1969) 'The Community-Centred School', in Gross, R. and Gross, B. *Radical School Reform*, Harmondsworth: Penguin.

Williams, B. (1985) *Ethics and the Limits of Philosophy*, London: Fontana.

Williams, R. (1961) *The Long Revolution*, Harmondsworth: Penguin.

Willis, P. (1977) *Learning to Labour: How Working Class Kids Get Working Class Jobs*, Sheffield: Saxon Press.

—— (1981) 'Cultural Production is Different from Cultural Reproduction ...', *Interchange*, 12(2–3): 48–67.

Wilson, J. D. (ed.) (1932) 'Introduction', in Arnold, M. (1869) *Culture and Anarchy*, 1963 edition, London: Penguin.

Wilson, V. and Woodhouse, J. (1990) *History Through Drama*, London: Historical Association.

Index